The Lay Ministry Revolution

Books by Eddy Hall

When Not to Build (with Ray Bowman)
Praying with the Anabaptists: The Secret of Bearing Fruit
  (with Marlene Kropf)

The Lay Ministry Revolution

How You Can Join

Eddy Hall and Gary Morsch

Baker Books

A Division of Baker Book House Co
Grand Rapids, Michigan 49516

© 1995 by Beacon Hill Press of Kansas City

Published by Baker Books
a division of Baker Book House Company
P.O. Box 6287, Grand Rapids, MI 49516-6287

This edition, published by Baker Book House in 1995, is a revision of *Ministry: It's Not Just For Ministers,* published by Beacon Hill Press in 1993.

Printed in the United States of America

Library of Congress Cataloging-in-Publication Data

Hall, Eddy.
    The lay ministry revolution : how you can join / Eddy Hall and
Gary Morsch.
      p. cm.
    ISBN 0-8010-9005-9 (pbk.)
    1. Lay ministry. 2. Lay ministry—Study and teaching. I. Morsch,
    Gary
BV677.H35 1995
253—dc20   95-11012

Contents

Foreword

During more than twenty years of pastoral ministry, I have often tried to fulfill the many expectations that go along with what I call a clergy-centered approach to ministry but have always ended up feeling frustrated and guilty. I never have enough time, never enough talent, never enough energy to fulfill all of the expectations. And, while feeling overwhelmed, I have often observed laypeople who are gifted and willing to serve but remain stifled and unfulfilled in their expressions of discipleship.

I believe that many of the frustrations of both overburdened pastoral staff and unfulfilled laity spring from the same source—the unbiblical division of God's people into categories of "ministers" and "non-ministers." And I feel strongly that the solution to both problems, and a key to the church's spiritual power, is to be found in the recovery of lay ministry.

In the hearts of all true believers, I am convinced, is a deep desire to do something significant for God and his kingdom in their lifetime. I have seen this in the lives of two of the strongest laypeople I have ever known. For as long as I can remember, my parents have given themselves to ministry, especially to the elderly. During my childhood I spent most Sunday afternoons with my family at the county-run "old folks home," where we sang and shared words of encouragement. I saw my parents visit these people regularly, plan activities and short trips for them, and give them daily care during times of critical need.

My parents are in their seventies now, but they are still going, still visiting, still ministering. They do it because God has given them this special calling, and through it they are fulfilling God's purposes. Far from being a burden, this ministry energizes and blesses them.

When I entered pastoral ministry, my parents' example was reinforced by the biblical injunction to pastors to "prepare God's people for works of service" (Eph. 4:12). Over the years I have had a growing desire to see those I pastor experience the same fulfillment in ministry that my parents enjoy. And so I have resolved to equip laity for, and release them into, ministry.

I confess, the effort has been neither easy nor quick to produce results. Releasing laity into ministry today is somewhat like releasing the Bible into the hands of the common people in Luther's day. Our roles as laypeople and clergy have become comfortable and familiar, even while they remain frustrating and unfulfilling. But I had caught a glimpse of the partnership in ministry that God intends for the church, and this glimpse kept me going through many years of seeing little response to this vision of shared ministry.

Now, after twenty-two years of pastoral ministry, something has broken through this "clergy-centered ministry" mind-set in the congregation I am pastoring. It is this course on lay ministry that you hold in your hands. I was preparing a series of sermons on the purposes of God for the lives and ministries of believers when I got a phone call from Eddy Hall asking whether our congregation would want to participate in developing a resource for lay ministry. What perfect timing! When I invited the people of my church to take part, forty eagerly responded. As we went through the pilot course together, I witnessed the freeing effects of the realization that every Christian is called to minister. I saw a growing fulfillment in those who began to live out this approach to ministry.

We have twice more offered this study to our congregation. I have now watched about 40 percent of our adults go through this course that helps people come to a biblical understanding of the nature of ministry, clarify their own calls, and live out those calls in everyday life. New ministries have sprung from some of these newly discovered calls, and still others are forming.

Recruiting and motivating laypeople to take on ministry responsibilities used to be one of my most difficult tasks. That aspect of my pastoring has changed since we started offering this class. More than half of those who have completed the class have come to me excitedly sharing their own sense of call. I no longer have to do any of the initial motivating. I only have to support and cheer on my lay ministers.

Do I believe that this book can help you? Oh, yes! Layperson, break free from the emptiness of not knowing where you fit into God's work. Pastor, trade in your frustration of being overwhelmed for the joy of multiplying your effectiveness through equipping others for ministry. Both, be the ministers God has called you to be!

Larry D. Morgan, senior pastor
First Church of the Nazarene
Newton, Kansas

To the forty-some ministers,
both professional and lay,
at the First Church of the Nazarene of Newton, Kansas,
who helped bring this book to life

Acknowledgments

We started work on this book with high hopes. It would be alive with compelling stories of real, ordinary laypeople involved in life-changing ministry. It would be fun, even exciting, to read. Above all, it would present truths about lay ministry in simple and practical ways, making them easy to understand and apply.

Once our outlining, research, and interviewing were done, but before much actual writing had taken place, that dream seemed in jeopardy. How could we be sure we were speaking to the real needs people felt, not just harping on our own pet themes? Were we overlooking important issues that thousands of laypeople would want to see addressed? Would the learning activities in the leaders guide really work in class sessions as they were intended to?

That's when Eddy called Pastor Larry Morgan at First Church of the Nazarene in Newton, Kansas, and asked, "Do you have a group of laypeople in your congregation who would be willing to take part in a pilot study of a book on lay ministry?" We couldn't have asked for a more cooperative or enthusiastic pastor. Such a study, he said, seemed to be perfectly timed with what God was already doing in the church.

Larry announced the upcoming study to his congregation, and about thirty people signed up. On five consecutive Sunday afternoons, from twenty to thirty laypeople met to explore the key concepts of this book together.

Once that group started meeting, there was no longer anything theoretical about writing the book. These were real people who intensely wanted to be used more effectively in ministry, and they had real questions. They described with amazing transparency both their hopes and frustrations concerning ministry. They responded to the teaching sometimes with enthusiasm for how helpful it was, other times pointing out how a poorly written story distracted them from what it was intended to teach. Some teaching methods proved amazingly effective; others had to be changed because they did not work as planned.

By the fifth week more than forty people had taken part in the class. At the close of our final session we stood in a circle, joined hands, and thanked God for the powerful way our visions for ministry had been broadened and how some of us had begun to discern our gifts and callings.

Much of the passion and urgency you will find in these pages, as well as a good deal of the clarity, is thanks to that group. Whatever ministry this book has, they have a part in it. And so the book is dedicated to Larry Morgan and those laypeople who played such a crucial role in shaping it.

The other group that made this book what it is are those who told us their stories. Many of those stories made it into print; many others did not, for lack of space or other reasons. But all contributed to making this a better book by giving us a pool of excellent stories from which to draw those best suited to our teaching goals.

Veteran editors Steve Miller and James N. Watkins graciously agreed to read the manuscript and offered many valuable suggestions to make the book more readable and accurate.

Most of all, we thank God, whose guidance and provision has been evident throughout the project, bringing together the right people at just the right time and providing extraordinary strength when the load of the work threatened to overwhelm. We now offer the book back to him to be used for his glory.

Welcome to the Revolution

Forty years ago Elton Trueblood wrote, "If the average church should suddenly take seriously the notion that every laymember—man or woman—is really a minister of Christ, we could have something like a revolution in a very short time."[1] Today, in church after church, his prediction is coming true.

The ministry of the laity is nothing new. It is as old as the gospel itself. The New Testament church was a great example of the ministry of all believers. While different believers had different ministries, each was expected to use his or her spiritual gifts for ministry, and the church flourished, spreading throughout the world.

In time, though, ministry became professionalized. The nonprofessionals, or laity, were relegated to a second-class status that all but locked them out of recognized ministry. This division of believers into two classes—"ministers" and "non-ministers"—persisted through the centuries. From time to time spiritual leaders such as Martin Luther attacked this heresy—and with some success. But it is only in our day, we believe, that the full harvest of their efforts in this area will be reaped.

Gary: Through my volunteer work I have had the privilege of meeting thousands of laypeople, in many countries.

I've found it exciting to witness the tremendous growth of so many churches. The churches outside North America are often growing faster than those within. Why are they growing so fast?

An essential part of the answer, I am convinced, is that in these churches the laypeople are full partners in ministry. They don't expect the pastor and staff to do the work of ministry for them. It is primarily the laypeople, supported by their pastors, who are reaching out and winning their communities for Christ. In many cases, in fact, it is laypeople who are planting the new churches.

I believe that the freeing of the laity now taking place in many denominations throughout the world has the potential to have an impact on our communities and our world for Christ in ways few, if any, of us can imagine. As the number of believers saying yes to God's call to ministry multiplies, and as the church equips and supports its members in fulfilling their calls, the church's effectiveness in carrying out its mission is also multiplying.

This book is an invitation to join this lay ministry revolution—an invitation not so much to you individually but to the laypeople in your church as a whole. Reading this book can expand your understanding of the nature of ministry, help you identify your spiritual gifts and calling, and give you ideas for how to move out into more effective ministry. And, of course, that would be tremendous.

However, this book will fully accomplish its purpose only when *congregations* use it as a tool to help *groups* of laypeople expand their understanding of ministry, to enable *groups* of laypeople to identify their spiritual gifts and callings, and to show laypeople how they can engage in more effective ministry *together*. The goal of this book is not merely personal spiritual renewal through moving into greater personal ministry, but congregational renewal. And so this book is designed primarily for group study and group action. The study/action guide at the back of this book gives the group leader clear, step-by-step instructions for guiding a group in his or her congregation through this experience.

This renewal in your congregation will likely start small—with an adult Sunday school class, a church board retreat, or a class created specifically to explore lay ministry. But when a nucleus of laypeople clearly discern and start living out their calls to ministry, their energy can be contagious. As more and more people catch the excitement, the study can be repeated with new groups of people until the dynamics of your congregation have been so transformed that you would describe it as nothing less than a lay ministry revolution.

Welcome to the revolution!

Over the centuries millions of Christians have believed a crippling myth: Ministry is just for "ministers." God's call to ministry, so the myth goes, comes only to the select few. The rest of us are laypeople by default, called only to receive ministry and support the ministries of others.

However, the Bible renounces this myth with an empowering truth: If I am a Christian, I am called to minister.

The Ministry Myth

G*ary:* When I was ten years old, this business of ministry all seemed so simple. As I listened to a sermon about being open to God's call to ministry, I believed that God was calling me. That morning I knelt and dedicated my life to whatever ministry God would call me to. Then I stood and announced, "God has called me to be a minister!"

In the months that followed, hardly a Wednesday night prayer meeting went by that I didn't stand and testify, "God has called me to be a minister." Afterward, supportive church members would encourage me. "You'll make a fine preacher, just like your daddy," they would say.

Then several months later, in another service, I once again felt God talking to me about my future. I did not hear an audible voice, but just as surely as I had earlier sensed that God wanted me to commit my life to ministry, I felt that God was impressing on me that I was to work in the field of science.

I was confused. Did God call people to more than one vocation? How could I be both a minister and a scientist? I took my confusion to my dad. "Dad, can a person be a minister and a scientist at the same time?"

My dad thought for a while, then responded, "Sure."

"What do they call someone who is both a minister and a scientist?"

"Well, let's see," my dad said. "I guess you would say God has called you to be a research minister."

I had no clue as to what a "research minister" was, but it sounded good to me. Thereafter, for many months on Wednesday nights, I testified that God had called me to be a research minister. (At least my dad did not say that God was calling me to be a Christian Scientist.) I repeated this testimony until an older Christian friend advised me that there really was no such thing as a research minister and pointed out that God surely intended for me to go into "the ministry."

Never again would I stand on a Wednesday night and say that God had called me into the ministry. Though my sense of call to ministry was as strong as ever, I had painfully learned that to mention my call publicly was to invite pressure from others to enter "the ministry"—to be a pastor, evangelist, or missionary. I did not believe that God was calling me to any of those vocations, but I could not explain to anyone else—or even to myself—how that could be true if God had, in fact, called me to be a minister. Rather than raise questions I couldn't answer, I just quit talking to other people about my call.

I had long assumed that when I graduated from high school I would go on to a Christian college. But when graduation time came I found that my inner struggle over God's call was paralyzing me. How could I go to college if I was confused about what God was leading me to do? How would I know how to prepare? Maybe I was mistaken and God really was calling me to be a pastor, missionary, or evangelist. But in my heart I knew I wasn't mistaken. God had called me to be a minister but in some other way, some way I hadn't yet been able to imagine.

Not Just for "Ministers"

My turmoil over my calling led me to do something unexpected for a good Christian kid who was supposed to be enrolling in a Christian college. I joined the army.

It seemed an unlikely choice. It was 1969, the Vietnam War was going strong, thousands of soldiers were dying, and seventeen-year-olds had to have their parents' permission to be sent off to war. But God can use anything, and he used my time in the military to begin showing me that I could minister without being in the professional ministry.

Wherever I was stationed, I became as involved as possible in a local church, teaching Sunday school or working with the youth group. While I was stationed at Fort Benning, Georgia, I even served as a supply pastor. Though I didn't fully realize it at the time, God was beginning to show me that being a layperson didn't keep me from being a minister. I came out of the army ready to attend college and prepare for the ministry—as a layperson.

I was beginning to understand that the reason for the confusion I had labored under for years was that I had believed what I now call the ministry myth: Ministry is just for "ministers," *ministers* here meaning only full-time ministry professionals.*

Though I didn't know what field God wanted me to enter, I did know I was going to college to prepare for ministry. So without declaring myself a religion major, I started taking religion courses while waiting for God to make his direction clear.

On campus, however, I found the ministry myth alive and well. Time and again well-meaning students and professors reminded me that a Christian serves God best as a ministry professional, not as a layperson. Chapel speakers often challenged us to say yes to God's call to full-time professional ministry, but rarely did they challenge us to respond to God's call to ministry as laypeople.

I gave God every opportunity to call me into full-time professional ministry. That is what everyone else seemed to expect of me, and I had come to expect it myself. But the call to be a pastor or missionary never came.

During a time of prayer and reflection in my junior year, I was searching for God's will for my future. More than ever, I sensed God's call to ministry, but I was also feeling led to change my major to premedicine. That surprised me. That was the one field I had secretly longed to enter, but I had never seriously considered it, because the ministry myth had convinced me that medicine was not real ministry. But God made clear to me that day that I was to minister through medicine. This call was confirmed when my pastor told me, "As a doctor you will have opportunities to minister to all kinds of people in the community that I will never be able to reach as a pastor." And so I spent the rest of my schooling preparing for ministry as a medical doctor.

---

* The Bible nowhere uses the word minister to refer exclusively to ministry professionals, so where it is used in that sense in this book it is enclosed in quotation marks.

The High Cost of the Myth

I wish my experience were unique, but in talking with other laypeople I am often reminded that it is not. The ministry myth has been so widely believed for so long that it has no doubt kept millions of Christians from seeing themselves as ministers and recognizing what God was calling them to do. This myth has paralyzed many and has crippled the ministries of others by causing them to misinterpret God's call.

My friend Mark knew that laypeople could minister, but he bought into the version of the ministry myth that says God can *best* use those who are in the professional ministry. Wanting to invest his whole life in ministry so that he could be as effective as possible for the kingdom of God, he quit his job, invested three years in a seminary education, and then joined a church staff.

In his new position Mark was responsible to equip people for ministry and to provide administrative support for the ministry of others. While he enjoyed much of the work, he quickly discovered that his gift was not administration. "I'm most effective in one-on-one ministry. And rather than coordinating existing ministries, I'd much rather be bringing new people in. I'd thought joining a church staff would give me more time for such things, but in fact it limited the time I could spend doing what I do best."

Mark resigned from his church staff job even though he knew that some people would misunderstand. "A lot of people might think that, having served on a church staff and now being in the insurance business, I've settled for 'God's second best.' But I now have far more opportunity for the ministry God has called me to.

"The passion of my life is to offer God's hope to broken people. Though I didn't realize it when I went into insurance, it is a perfect job for someone who wants to work with hurting people. Whenever an elderly client loses a spouse, I get a phone call. When any of my clients divorce, they have to come to me to change their insurance papers. And, of course, whenever one of them has a car accident, a fire, or a serious illness covered by a policy I carry, the client comes to see me.

"My work gives me lots of opportunities to sit down and talk with people in crisis. Most of them don't know Christ, and I often have the chance to share with them the source of my hope. Just a few weeks ago I told my wife that I've never before felt God using me in ministry like I have lately."

The ministry myth led Mark into a professional ministry position for which he was not gifted and which actually limited his contact with the people to whom God was calling him to minister. It was only when he understood that God could use him more effectively as a layperson than as a professional minister that God was able to put Mark's ministry gifts to fullest use.

The Myth's Origin

For centuries much of the church has divided itself into two groups—the clergy, or "ministers," and the laity, the ones ministered to. Where did this historic division within the church come from? Does it find its roots in Scripture?

Not at all. The New Testament clearly teaches that God has given every Christian one or more spiritual gifts with which to minister. Paul wrote to the Corinthians, "There are different kinds of gifts, but the same Spirit. . . . To each one the manifestation of the Spirit is given for the common good" (1 Cor. 12:4, 7). Peter wrote, "Serve one another with whatever gift each of you has received" (1 Peter 4:10 NRSV). Though in the Old Testament only a select group of God's people served as priests, in the New Testament church all believers are priests—mediators between God and the rest of the people (1 Peter 2:5, 9). We are all called to offer God's love and forgiveness to other people and to take the needs and concerns of other people to God.

One pastor writes, "There is no room in the New Testament church for a hierarchy of callings. There is no biblical or theological justification for regarding church leaders as peculiarly called of God to minister holy things or to be 'full-time' for God, while considering the layperson, who serves God in both church and world, as having a lesser call or no call at all. The call of God comes to every believer who has ears to hear."[2]

God does call certain people to leadership in the church, and their role is essential to the church's vitality and effectiveness. But, in describing the call of leaders, Scripture does not single them out as the "ministers." Rather, it emphasizes the ministry of all believers: "The gifts he gave were that some would be apostles, some prophets, some evangelists, some pastors and teachers, *to equip the saints for the work of ministry*" (Eph. 4:11–12 NRSV, emphasis added). The call of these church leaders, then, is not to do the work of ministry so that we don't have to, but to equip *us* to do ministry.

Gordon Cosby, pastor of the Church of the Saviour in Washington, D.C., says it this way: "The primary task of the professional minister [is] training nonprofessional ministers for their ministry."[3]

Although the New Testament teaches that all believers are ministers, over the centuries a separation between "ministers" (clergy) and "non-ministers" (laity) has developed and widened. A fourth-century church document stated that the laity should merely "sit and say amen."[4] In A.D. 619 a church council ruled that the laity and clergy should remain separate. They based their ruling on Deuteronomy 22:10, which states that an ox and a donkey should not plow together.[5]

Throughout history there have been many attempts to correct this unbiblical division. Of these, the Protestant Reformation, sparked in 1517 when Martin Luther posted his ninety-five theses on the Wittenberg church door, is the best known. In reaffirming "the priesthood of all believers" Luther had simply rediscovered a biblical truth, that God has "made us to be . . . priests" (Rev. 1:6).

Signs of Hope

The fact that today we are still needing to talk about reclaiming ministry for all believers shows that the work of the Reformation is not yet complete. But there are signs of hope.

More and more Christians are realizing that we are all called to minister. People who have never before seen themselves as ministers are now saying, "Yes, I am a minister." One clergyman has written that the notion that all ministry is done by the pastors is "as dead as last year's bird's nest."[6]

This pronouncement may be a bit optimistic, but even if the myth that ministry is just for "ministers" is not quite dead, it clearly is dying. In recent years we have seen more and more laity taking up ministry. Pastors are reclaiming their biblical role of equipping believers for ministry. Because they know that the church can never fulfill its mission so long as only a handful of leaders do the work, they are trying to mobilize every believer in the church. As laypeople embrace their calls to minister and pastors give priority to equipping them for ministry, we are all learning to work together as ministry partners in new and creative ways.

It is only as we recognize that each of us is called to minister, and as each of us says yes to that call, that the church can fulfill its mission to be the hands and feet of Christ in a hurting world.

M inistry in its purest and simplest form is love.
... Ministry is, in fact, doing love!

Win Arn

2

Washing Dirty Feet

It was a holy moment. Instituting the Lord's Supper, Jesus
had just offered his disciples the bread, representing his
body, and the cup, representing his blood. It was his last meal
with his disciples before his death. He would soon be taken
from them. And what did the disciples do? They argued. "A
dispute arose among them as to which of them was considered to be greatest" (Luke 22:24).

Probably in response to this dispute, Jesus silently rose
from the table, took off his robe, and wrapped a towel around
his waist, taking on the appearance of a slave. "After that, he
poured water into a basin and began to wash his disciples'
feet, drying them with the towel that was wrapped around
him" (John 13:5).

The roads of Palestine were dusty in dry weather and
muddy when it was wet. The sandals most people wore offered little protection against dust and mud. So by the door
of each house stood a large water pot, and as guests came
in, a servant would meet them with a pitcher and a towel to
wash their feet.

Since Jesus and his disciples had no servant, they must have normally shared this duty among themselves. But this night, perhaps because of the competitive spirit among them, no one washed feet—until Jesus rose to do it.

When he had finished, Jesus put his robe back on, again taking on the appearance of a rabbi, and returned to his place. "Now that I, your Lord and Teacher, have washed your feet," he said, "you also should wash one another's feet" (John 13:14).

Those words still call to us across the centuries. Not only does God call us to address spiritual needs (the ministry of the rabbi), but he also calls us to meet even the simplest of physical needs—needs others may consider unworthy of their attention (the ministry of the slave). To follow Jesus is to minister to both kinds of needs.

What Needs?

Eddy: During my college years I knew that even as a layperson I was called to minister. But ministry, as I understood it, involved meeting only spiritual needs.

While I was growing up, my Christianity had consisted mainly of observing a list of dos and don'ts. Do go to church faithfully. Don't steal or lie. Do read your Bible and pray every day. Don't smoke or drink. Do pay your tithe. Don't go to dances or movies. Do obey your parents. Don't fight with your brother or sister. If I could just follow all the dos and refrain from all the don'ts, I believed, then I would be a "good Christian."

One afternoon, probably during my sophomore year in high school, I lay on my bed mentally running through my checklist. I felt reassured by my high score. I was observing all the dos and avoiding all the don'ts—except for one. (The one about not fighting with siblings just might have slipped my mind that day.) The one thing I knew I was not doing that was required of a good Christian was witnessing.

The thought of trying to witness terrified me, probably mostly because I was so shy, but the thought of going to hell terrified me even more. Since I was convinced I had to witness to be a good Christian, I resolved to begin doing so.

The next year at school I organized a Bible club. Over the next two years the club conducted on-campus Bible studies, handed out evangelistic tracts, placed Bibles in every classroom, and sponsored morning devotions over the intercom. I confidently checked off the last item on my "good Christian" checklist.

When I was away at college, my witnessing usually took the form of going to a park on Sunday afternoons—with several other Christian college students—and approaching strangers with "The Four Spiritual Laws," a booklet that explained how to become a Christian. A half dozen or so of the people I talked to prayed the sinner's prayer. One even came to church afterward for a few months.

In time, however, we grew uneasy with our cold-turkey approach to witnessing. One reason was that we saw little evidence that it was leading to changed lives. But part of my discomfort, I believe, stemmed from my own changing relationship with God. Nurtured by my pastor's sermons, I was seeing God less as a critical judge—making a list and checking it twice—and more as a loving Father. I was beginning to realize that God was not only concerned about my getting to heaven; he also cared about my joys and pains, my hopes and fears. He was willing to guide me when I was confused, provide for me when I was in need, strengthen me when I was weak, and comfort me when I grieved. God didn't care only about my soul; he cared about me as a whole person.

The more I experienced God's love, the clearer it became that I was not treating my witnessing prospects the way God treated me. I was treating them as objects, as trophies to be won, not as hurting people who needed to be loved.

Somehow, early on, I had gotten the idea that ministry involved meeting only—or at least primarily—spiritual needs. Evangelizing, preaching, teaching the Bible, praying, spiritual counseling, leading worship—this was ministry. But feeding the hungry? Visiting the sick? Welcoming strangers? If you had asked me, I probably would have put such activities in the same category as joining the Boy Scouts—perhaps nice to do but hardly something God expected. I had not yet learned to see the dirty feet in my world.

However, as love replaced law as my motivation for ministry, I started seeing other people through new eyes. I became less concerned with persuading others to do the right thing and more concerned with meeting their needs. With this change in motivation it also became obvious to me that ministry had to be concerned not just with spiritual needs but with the needs of the total person. Love, I was beginning to see, can't limit itself to caring about only one kind of need.

This growing awareness that God's love compels us to respond to the needs of the whole person would eventually lead our family to join two others in moving to a low-income, inner-city neighborhood to share the gospel through ministries that responded to both spiritual and social needs. We held backyard Bible schools, helped to run a shelter for homeless families, taught English as a second language, and started a prayer and Bible study group. After a couple of years our family started taking in homeless families for periods of up to several months as we tried to help them stabilize their lives. Ten years later, some of those people still write or call us to ask for prayer and spiritual counsel.

Jesus Our Model

Jesus ministered to every conceivable kind of need. He forgave sins, healed the sick, taught his disciples, and championed the oppressed. In a society that saw women as vastly inferior, he treated women and men with equal respect. In a synagogue, while surrounded by racist Jews, he proclaimed God's equal love for Gentiles, even though he must have known that his audience would try to kill him (Luke 4:25–29). Jesus spent so much time with people whom others looked down on that his enemies branded him the "friend of tax collectors and 'sinners'" (Matt. 11:19).

Jesus calls us to respond to people's needs in the same way he did. "I was hungry and you gave me something to eat," he said, "I was thirsty and you gave me something to drink, I was a stranger and you invited me in, I needed clothes and you clothed me, I was sick and you looked after me, I was in prison and you came to visit me. . . . Whatever you did for one of the least of these brothers of mine, you did for me" (Matt. 25:35–36, 40). Especially amazing to those of us who grew up seeing such actions as optional are Jesus' words that those who do such things will receive eternal life and those who do not will receive eternal punishment (v. 46).

God calls us to minister to both spiritual and social needs. To respond to one and not the other is to fail to love as God loves. It is to fail to live out the gospel.

Behold, How They Love

In the first century non-Christians would remark of Christians, "Behold, how they love one another." Today when Christians respond with love to people in need, the world still takes notice.

On the last Sunday of 1991, while on his way to church, Steve Lamb was involved in a car accident in which he sustained a serious head injury. He was rushed to Mercy Hospital in Oklahoma City, where he lay in a coma. From the hospital, Steve's wife, Cyndi, called their church, where the morning service was in progress.

"People from our church came to the hospital and stayed with me all day long," Cyndi says. As people left to go home that night, Cyndi faced the prospect of spending the night alone as she waited for updates on Steve's condition. At about ten o'clock her friend Debbie showed up with blankets and pillows and announced, "I'm here to camp out with you."

Cyndi remembers, "From that day until Steve was transferred to an out-of-state hospital in April, every weekday someone from the church came to the hospital to be with me. Twice a week people from the church would bring us meals, usually enough food to make four meals. Once a week someone would come by to do my grocery shopping and run errands for me. Since we lived in Edmond and the church is in Bethany, this wasn't convenient for any of them. They all lived thirty minutes away."

Although this assistance was coordinated through sign-up sheets at the church, it was initiated entirely by laypeople, not by church staff. That impressed Cyndi.

The people of the church have not only given practical assistance but also offered their prayers. Within a few weeks of the accident one woman in the church started hosting a weekly prayer meeting for Steve and the family.

During those first weeks after the accident, Cyndi remembers thinking, "This is wonderful, but will anyone be here in a month?" The weeks of hospitalization turned into months, but the caring support of Christian friends continued.

The Lambs had excellent medical insurance but no disability insurance, leaving the family with no income. Cyndi's friends didn't want her to have to go to work right away. They felt she needed to be free to take care of her sons, Jeremy and Tate, ages eleven and six, and regularly spend time with Steve at the hospital. Besides, a baby was on the way, and they wanted her to be able to stay at home with the baby.

"God has met our financial needs in two ways," Cyndi explains. "First, people began giving us services at no charge—dental and medical care, haircuts, oil changes, car repairs. One man in our church gave me a credit card and told me to charge all my gasoline to that card. Another church member who has a landscaping business added me to his route but didn't charge me. He did all kinds of things for our lawn that we had never done before. We had the best-looking lawn in Edmond.

"About February a couple of men set up a fund for our family at the church and sent out a letter asking people to give to it. Now I just take my bills to the church, and the church pays them out of that fund. There's always been more than enough to meet our needs. I haven't had to spend one moment worrying about finances.

"Of all that people have done," says Cyndi, "most meaningful to me as a mother is what people have done for my children. From the beginning, several families have gone out of their way to include my boys in what they are doing. For example, Christmas vacation, the first anniversary of the accident, was an especially difficult time for us. Though it had been a full year after the accident, people were still going out of their way to include my boys. A man from the church took Jeremy and Tate bowling with his boys. The next day another family took them horseback riding with their girls. The next day it was an invitation to a science museum, and the next day an invitation to watch a ball game on big-screen TV. They've been taken to rodeos, on camp-outs and fishing trips, and to college football games."

Being dependent on the generosity of others can be hard for anyone. Cyndi remembers, "When this happened I felt like God said to me, 'You're not going to make it unless you can let others help you.' I realized I could no longer keep tabs, so I've been able to relax and freely accept God's lavish provision."

Steve came home from the hospital in November 1993, almost two years after the accident. He gets around with the help of a motorized wheelchair and has regained full use of his right hand. Grateful to be alive, he is almost always in good spirits.

Even three years after the accident, the church's support is as strong as ever. Contributions to the fund set up at the church have continued to be more than enough to meet the Lambs' financial needs. The weekly prayer group continues to meet. People were still bringing in meals two and a half years after the accident, when Cyndi asked them to stop, preferring to do her own cooking again.

The church's outpouring of love to the Lambs is a powerful example of ministry to the whole person—ministering to spiritual, financial, practical, and emotional needs—but the Lambs are not the only ones who have been ministered to in the process.

Cindy Penick works as a secretary for Mark, one of the people coordinating the help for the Lambs. For a year before Steve's accident Mark had been inviting her to church, but she had never come. In the period immediately after the accident, as many as ten people a day would call Mark at the office to check on Steve's condition or offer help. People would come by the office, and Cindy was amazed at how much they cared.

"Mark told me how people were giving out of their pockets to help the Lambs, but I didn't believe it," Cindy says. "There was no way people could give like that without wanting to get something out of it for themselves."

So impressed was Cindy that the next time Mark invited her to church, she agreed to go, but she was still skeptical. She could not believe what she was hearing. "But," says Cindy, "the first Sunday, people were so welcoming and loving, I went back. In the coming weeks, the more I heard what people were doing for the Lambs, the more overwhelmed I was."

Cindy and her children have been going to church ever since. In fact, she has joined the church and found her own ministry role in working in the church nursery. Most important, though, is that for the first time in her life God is real and personal to her. "God had always been distant to me. I didn't know I could talk to God. Now he's a personal friend. And the change I've seen in my family this last year has been truly amazing. I feel like I've found a home."

Win Arn, a leader in the church growth movement, writes, "Ministry in its purest and simplest form is love.... Ministry is, in fact, doing love!"[7] When we respond to hurting people with loving, whole-person ministry, the world cannot help but notice, and people will be drawn to Christ.

A Liberating Call

Is it good news to hear that God calls us to minister not just to spiritual needs but to all kinds of needs? Or does it sound as though God is expecting you to do more than you can possibly do? It *could* sound that way. But the good news is that while God does call us to respond to every kind of need, he doesn't expect any of us to do it alone.

While no one person can effectively reach out to every kind of need, all of us working together *can!* God has placed within the body of Christ all the spiritual gifts needed to minister to the many needs both within the church and in the world around us.

Far from being burdensome, the call to whole-person ministry can be liberating to people whose understanding of ministry has been limited to meeting spiritual needs. Because they are not gifted in evangelism or Bible teaching or spiritual counseling or any of the other areas of ministry that focus primarily on spiritual needs, some deeply committed Christians have spent years feeling guilty and frustrated about their personal ministries.

Often the reason for their frustration is simple: God has given them abilities that minister primarily to other kinds of needs. If your spiritual gift is serving, you may find joy in helping other people by repairing cars or buildings, by lending a hand at the time of a move, by cleaning, by running errands. If it is showing mercy, you may be best at taking meals to shut-ins, caring for the sick or disabled, or visiting nursing home residents. If encouragement is your gift, you may be good at supporting someone through a crisis or motivating others to do what's right even when it is difficult. Maybe your gift is giving to meet others' needs. You may not be very good at any of these things yet be gifted at coordinating the efforts of those who are.

Think of what a crucial role each of these spiritual gifts played in ministering to the Lambs. No one person could have met such a wide range of needs, but by working together the body of Christ met all the needs.

If you have had trouble finding your niche in ministry, could it be because your definition of ministry has been too narrow? Can you think of one way God uses you to meet another person's need? Any kind of need? If you can, you have just named one way you minister.

Moustapha's first contact with The Lamb's Center, a church-related outreach located just off New York's Times Square, was the time he came into the health clinic asking for cough medicine. The doctor gave him the medicine, then asked, "Do you need anything else?"

"Yeah, I'm on drugs," Moustapha answered.

"Do you want to get off?"

"Of course, I want off. But who can get off drugs?" Moustapha wanted to know.

The doctor's next question took the patient completely by surprise. "Do you know Christ?"

"What does Christ have to do with this?" Moustapha asked. The idea that Christianity could help him with his drug problem was totally foreign to him.

Moustapha had been born and raised in a Muslim family in Senegal, West Africa. His father, who had eight wives, was the head of his tribal village. Of his fifty or sixty children, Moustapha had been one of his favorites, and as a child Moustapha had studied the Koran so that he could succeed his father as the village's spiritual leader.

Later his brother had loaned him money so that he could come to the United States to study business and then return to Senegal to work in his brother's business. But while in school Moustapha had started using and pushing drugs, exhausted his brother's money, and found himself living on the streets. By the time he came into The Lamb's Center clinic, he had been living on the streets of New York for several years.

Although the idea of Christ being able to help him with his drug addiction was totally new to him, a few weeks after the doctor's invitation Moustapha attended church for the first time. Two to three months later, he accepted Christ.

He immediately got involved in the church's discipleship program. The church offered him housing at The Lamb's Center in exchange for work in the counseling center. On Pentecost Sunday, 1991, Moustapha was baptized. He is now working full-time for the church—part-time with social services and part-time with counseling services. For Moustapha, Christianity is good news.

David Best, the pastor who baptized Moustapha, has a simple definition of ministry. "Ministry is loving people like Jesus would. It is serving people in God's name so that he gets the glory."

God calls each of us to different kinds of ministry, but he calls all of us to wash dirty feet. Who are the hurting people whose lives you can touch with God's love? What needs do you see going unmet because not enough people care? Where in your world are the dirty feet?

Will you say yes to God's call to be a foot washer?

A lone man, a pastor, stands in a church sanctuary, surrounded by empty seats. "The church is most the church," he says into the camera, "when the sanctuary is empty."[8] James Garlow, pastor of the Metroplex Chapel in Dallas–Fort Worth, is tackling yet another myth—that most of the church's ministry takes place when the church is gathered.

3

The Empty Sanctuary

One night in July 1987 Jim Couchenour got a phone call that would change the outward course of his life. For many years Jim had invested himself wholeheartedly in the work of the church. In his local congregation he was a board member, chairman of the finance committee, head of the development committee, and a member of the choir. On the district level he served on the advisory board and the finance committee. He was on the board of trustees of a church college. And on the denominational level he served on the general board and various commissions. Here, in his own words, is Jim's story of how that evening phone call sparked a radical change in his approach to ministry:

Sam,[9] a close friend of mine who had a drinking problem, had gotten upset at home that evening and stormed out of the house. His wife, Diane, was afraid he was headed for the tavern. She called to ask whether I would please go look for him. Of course I told her I would.

I put on my jeans and went down to the town's only tavern. Not sure I wanted anyone to see me going in, I went around to the back. I walked up to a woman sitting by the back door and said, "I'm looking for a fellow named Sam."

"He's not here," she said. "Furthermore, he's not going to be here. He owes me $123 for a bar bill, and the police know he's not to be admitted back in here again."

I thanked her and left.

I didn't find Sam that night, but as I prayed that evening and the next morning, God laid a strange request on me. I was to go back down to the tavern and offer to pay Sam's bar bill.

Now, I was raised in a parsonage. I've been in the church all my life, and I'd never been in a tavern before. That would be the first bar bill I'd ever paid.

I went back that night and asked for Nellie. I'd heard she operated the tavern. Someone pointed to a woman sitting on a barstool and playing cards with the bartender. It was the same woman I'd met the night before.

I sat down on the stool next to her and introduced myself.

"I remember you from last night," she said.

"Nellie," I said, "I'm here partly because I'm concerned about my friend Sam, but I also know you have a business to run. I have some cash here and I'd like to pay something on Sam's bar bill." I gave her the ninety dollars I had in my pocket, and she thanked me.

I sat for twenty minutes that night talking to Nellie Watson. I found out that this 65-year-old lady, way back in her early childhood, had gone to Sunday school. She'd even taught Sunday school once and had a vague belief in prayer.

I left that night, not expecting ever to go back again. But God had other ideas. The next morning as I prayed, God laid on my heart a ridiculous request—that I go back down to Nellie's and ask her whether she would let a gospel-singing group put on a concert in the tavern some Saturday night.

That night I was back in the tavern. "Nellie," I said, "I think you really care about the people who come in here, and I do too, but I don't know them. I don't think they'd ever come to church, but how would you feel about us bringing a religious singing group down here and putting on a concert?"

She sat there for a moment, then said, "That's a great idea."

A week from that following Saturday night, five people from our local church went down to Young's Tavern and for two hours sang to that tavern crowd. It was one of the most fascinating evenings of my life. Nellie would get my attention and point to someone. I'd go over and sit on the barstool alongside the person, and within ninety seconds he or she would be sharing important life concerns. We'd talk a little bit; then Nellie would get my attention and point to someone else. I'd go to the next person, and the same thing would happen. Over and over again that night, we dispensed Philippians 4:4–7: "Rejoice in the Lord always. . . . Do not be anxious about anything, but in everything, by prayer and petition, with thanksgiving, present your requests to God. And the peace of God, which transcends all understanding, will guard your hearts and your minds in Christ Jesus."

The next Wednesday I went back. As I walked through the back door, Nellie said, "Oh boy, am I glad to see you. Here's a fellow I want you to talk to. John, get over here. This is the guy I was telling you about." Then she explained, "John here is trying to quit drinking, but he needs to know where to go to AA meetings, and I figured you could help him." Well, I knew nothing about Alcoholics Anonymous meetings, but I did talk to John and we were later able to direct him to an AA group.

Every Wednesday for the next six months, rather than going to church for prayer meeting, I went back to the tavern. Every single Wednesday night either someone was waiting for me or someone came in while I was there, wanting help for a problem. I kind of became the chaplain of Young's Tavern, and other Christians from my church got involved in the ministry as well.

Along about September, one of the fellows at the tavern said, "I wish we had more time to talk." So we started going back to the tavern after church on Sunday nights to talk with whoever wanted to talk about spiritual things. I have never found it so easy to share about God and his love.

At Christmastime one of the men of the church provided a full-course dinner free of charge to the tavern people. That night we held another Christian concert.

In January 1988 Nellie closed the tavern both for financial reasons and because of a growing awareness that she shouldn't be involved in this sort of thing. When the tavern closed, we kept the Wednesday and Sunday night sessions going in homes. One cold February evening in a small-group meeting, Nellie Watson gave her heart to Jesus Christ.

The lady who had operated the bar before Nellie had taken it over was a friend of Nellie's. Nellie invited her to church and she came. She recommitted her life to God and is now a member of our church. The same thing began happening in other people's lives.

In July God told me to resign from the church board. I had no idea why God was telling me to do that after all these years. But God knew. He knew that in the fall we would find the building he had in mind for a ministry that would open in December.[10]

Today, what started as a tavern ministry has grown into a multifaceted outreach in Columbiana, Ohio, called The Way Station. In a building near the former tavern Jim and other volunteers installed pool tables, a foosball table, a pinball machine, and other games. The Way Station is open seven nights a week from 7:00 P.M. until 1:00 A.M. In addition to the nightly drop-in fellowship, the center sponsors support groups for drug addicts, survivors of sexual abuse, adults raised in dysfunctional homes, and people with eating disorders. There are Bible studies, prayer meetings, English-as-a-second-language classes, programs for children and retired persons, and concerts. Emergency transportation, food and clothing, and a crisis referral service are always available. The Way Station is now staffed by more than thirty volunteers and a full-time youth minister.

Jim says:

> God introduced us to the world of dilated eyes of marijuana, the flaring nostrils of cocaine, financial needs, and other burdens that most of us cannot comprehend. He showed me that this world is going to hell without us laypeople doing what God wants us to do. I've lived in Columbiana twenty-eight years. All these needs, all these problems, all this hopelessness was there all the time that I was living with my nice family, my nice church people, my nice committee people. Right in my hometown there was a mission field as cross-cultural as any mission field in the world.[11]

Jim would eventually resign from all but one of the church boards and commissions he had served on before The Way Station started, but his story doesn't mean that everyone who holds a position in the church should resign from it and start a ministry in the community. It does, though, show the danger the church faces of becoming ingrown and being content with maintaining its traditional ministries while all around it hurting people are crying out for help. And Jim's story demonstrates that we all need to let the Holy Spirit create within us a sensitivity to people's needs, wherever they are.

Purpose of the Church Gathered

In many congregations the ministries of the church scattered have received less attention than the ministries of the church gathered. "Perhaps the greatest threat [to] the Christian Church today," writes James Garlow, "is the threat of 'ingrownness,' so focusing on itself and its own needs that it fails to remember the purpose for which it was called into existence."[12] Some churches have, in fact, become ingrown. They have forgotten that one critical reason for coming together is to become equipped for ministry, so that each member can then go out to minister every day of the week.

In some ways the church is like a sales team. When the sales team meets, its members may celebrate recent accomplishments. Sales managers may try to inspire and motivate the team, to give them a vision of what is possible. Group members may encourage one another or empathize with each other's difficulties. This all helps to build a sense of community; group members feel they are not alone, but part of a team. Some meetings include training to equip each salesperson to do a more effective job.

Now what would you think of that sales team if, upon leaving the meeting, the members made little or no effort to sell? Would you suspect that they missed the point of the meeting?

We in the church are not a sales team but a ministry team, yet we gather for many of the same reasons—to celebrate, to expand our vision, to be inspired to fulfill our mission, to give and receive encouragement, and to become equipped for ministry. If then, at the end of our gathering, we go out into the world but make little attempt to minister, what does that suggest? Could it be that we missed the point of why we came together?

Eddy: I recently visited an adult Sunday school class and came away convinced that the teacher and class officers knew exactly why the class came together every Sunday. To begin with, they came together for fellowship and mutual encouragement. Their class calendar showed several upcoming fellowship events outside the Sunday morning time slot. Many members had been together in the class for years and had formed deep friendships. The class was fulfilling many of the New Testament commands to minister to one another. But this class came together for more than fellowship.

If you had been with me that morning, you would have heard one class member describe how we often give gifts to poor children at Christmas but overlook the fact that poor children may have nothing to give to their parents. For years this class had supported a local shelter for homeless families with their money, many hours of volunteer work, and their love. This Christmas, class members were being invited to buy gifts that children at the shelter could, in turn, give to their parents.

You would have heard another class member make an announcement about the visitation schedule for a husband and wife who were serving prison sentences for acts they had committed before becoming Christians. So many people from the church—about half of them from this one class—were visiting this couple that the prison would not permit more names to be added to the visitation list. But, the class member explained, it was possible to rotate people on and off the list. A prayer request for the husband was shared, and class members were reminded to send cards to the wife on her birthday.

You would have heard a Sunday school lesson about ministering to family members, one that was not merely theoretical but called for specific application.

The teacher of that class understood that her job was not simply to teach the Sunday school lesson but to equip her class members to wash dirty feet, to minister seven days a week to people in need wherever they were—within the church, within their families, in their communities, or in the world beyond their communities.

Ministry within the Church

Though most ministry takes place when the church is scattered, not gathered, our ministry is to begin within the

Christian family. Paul wrote, "Whenever we have an opportunity, let us work for the good of all, and *especially for those of the family of faith*" (Gal. 6:10 NRSV, emphasis added).

We all are ministered to by others in the family of faith. Most of us who grew up in the church can look back on Sunday school teachers whose love and caring made a lasting difference in our lives. We appreciate the pianist and organist and choir members who help us worship each Sunday. We depend on janitors and gardeners to make the church building and grounds look cared for and welcoming. Ushering and greeting, far from being simple chores, can have powerful effects when approached as ministries.

Bill Harris's days as a greeter began one Sunday morning more than thirty-five years ago. When he noticed that someone needed help finding a chair in his crowded Sunday school class, he jumped up and showed the person a seat. He has been a greeter ever since. For the past thirteen years he has been greeting people at the curbside as they arrive for church.

"I've always wanted to make people feel comfortable and at home," Bill says. "If I notice someone standing alone in a crowd, I'll often go up and talk to him." Bill has the important ministry of making people feel welcome.

When the church gathers, we depend on the ministries of all these people and more. But what if your gifts don't fit any of these particular roles? Do you have a ministry within the body of Christ?

Indeed you do. We all do. We all can minister within the body of Christ, whatever our gifts. This is because most ministry in the body does not involve carrying out the responsibilities of a position. It comes through simple acts of caring, one person to another.

The "one another" commands of the New Testament—be devoted to one another, accept one another, serve one another, bear one another's burdens, encourage one another, love one another, and many more—all describe how we are to relate to fellow believers. I can minister with a hug on Sunday morning or an encouraging phone call during the week. Saying, "I'll pray for you," then doing it; babysitting so that parents can have a night out; and putting an anonymous gift in the mail to help with a medical bill are all examples of ministry. The first Christian church described in Acts did such a good job of caring for each other's material needs that it was said of them, "There were no needy persons among them" (4:34). Can that be said of your church?

Ministering to each other's personal needs, all kinds of needs, as an expression of the love God gives us for one another is at the very heart of authentic church life. One bumper sticker reads, "Practice random acts of kindness and senseless acts of beauty." It is these daily acts of love that bind us together and show the world that we are Jesus' followers.

Ministry to Your Family

Not all of us have spouses or children, but those without usually have other family nearby or family-like relationships. For people who are serious about ministry, it is sometimes tempting to get caught up in ministry within the church, in the community, or across the ocean, and shortchange our ministry to those who sit around our kitchen table.

Eddy: I loved my work as director of an inner-city ministry organization. Almost every morning I woke up excited about going to the office, eager to plunge into the work of planning, counseling, and teaching.

Though my wife tried to tell me so, it wasn't until I had left that job that I realized how much I had neglected my own family during those years. I had not been the kind of husband or father my family needed. I realized I had to find a way to make ministry to my family a higher priority than my work. I had been thinking of returning to inner-city ministry but concluded that I needed a job that demanded less of my time and energy, at least while our children were young.

I got a job as a secretary. To go from being the director of a ministry organization to being a secretary is not the kind of career move the world applauds—or even understands—but it was a decision God honored.

Within a few months I was able to cut my secretarial job back to four days a week to spend one day a week on my writing. A year later my freelance writing business had grown to the point that I could resign my secretarial job and write full-time.

Today I enjoy writing just as much as I enjoyed inner-city ministry, and it seldom takes more than forty hours a week. Best of all, because I work at home I am able to help home school our children, and I can be there for my family whenever I'm needed.

Making ministry to family a top priority has its costs—sometimes in career advancement, sometimes in income, sometimes in both. But the rewards are beyond anything money can buy.

Ministry to Your Community

Shortly after Roy Eagan sold his plumbing business to retire, he went to the administrator of the Children's Convalescent Center in Bethany, Oklahoma, a center for the long-term care of seriously handicapped children, and told him, "I'm here to work." While doing plumbing work for the center earlier, Roy had noticed some maintenance needs going unmet. Now that he had time he wanted to volunteer.

When Roy offered his help, the administrator told his secretary, "Lock the door and get a time card!" And that's how Roy became the new maintenance person—part paid, part volunteer—at the convalescent center.

Roy became much more than a maintenance person, however. Working day after day among handicapped children separated from their families, he became the resident "papa" for many of the children.

On Roy's seventy-fifth birthday the children at the center threw him a party. One four-year-old girl, on behalf of all the children, gave him a shirt. On the front it says, "Super Papa." And on the back: "He works for hugs."

Local organizations such as food pantries, shelters for the homeless, and crisis-pregnancy centers are good places to find "dirty feet." Many churches operate ministries of community outreach such as Meals-on-Wheels, Mothers' Day Out, and after-school programs for latchkey children.

Some Christians minister by serving on school boards or in local government. Others participate in civic organizations and professional societies. We may be inclined to view such involvements as taking time away from ministry because they are not church related. While God will not lead every Christian to join such organizations, participation in them can provide opportunities to build relationships with others in our communities and minister to their needs.

Ministry to the World

Sometimes what starts out as a local ministry grows to have a broader impact. Gary and Janalee Hoffman sensed God's call to begin visiting inmates at a medium security prison in Jean, Nevada. That ministry expanded after Henry, one of Gary's former employees, was convicted of murder and sentenced to Nevada's death row. Before Henry started serving his sentence, he committed his life to the Lord. Shortly after arriving on death row he started asking Gary and Jan for Christian literature to give to his fellow prisoners in Carson City. Soon Gary and Jan found themselves corresponding with most of the thirty-six men on Nevada's death row.

The Hoffmans were surprised to discover twelve believers on death row, but dismayed to learn that because of their workload, prison chaplains rarely visited these Christian brothers. The men were physically separated from each other and isolated from any personal ministry. Janalee began praying for a way to help bring these men together so that they could encourage one another. The plan the Lord gave was for a Christian newsletter written for and by death row convicts. The ministry of "The Rising Son" newsletter, initially for the men on Nevada's death row, has expanded rapidly. It now reaches six thousand prisoners in 152 penitentiaries, in all fifty states of the United States and in thirty-two other countries.

The Heart to Heart project is another ministry that started small, then mushroomed. Spearheaded by a group of laypeople through a local civic club, it began as a limited effort to gather medicines and medical supplies for the people of the former Soviet Union. To the great surprise of the organizers, the project gained the support of thousands of people throughout the American Midwest as well as the interest of the media. Grocery stores sponsored drives to collect donated over-the-counter medicines, and pharmaceutical companies pitched in. Over ninety tons of medicines and supplies were donated—with a value of over $5 million. The U.S. Air Force provided its largest plane, the C-5 Galaxy, to airlift the donations to Moscow, where they were distributed to hospitals and clinics.

Though the original organizers envisioned only one airlift, because of the outpouring of support two thousand Heart to Heart volunteers have gone on to gather and distribute more than four hundred tons of medical supplies and one thousand tons of food—with a wholesale value of more than $47 million—to needy people in Albania, Bulgaria,

Croatia, Kazahkstan, China, Ethiopia, Ukraine, Bosnia, Vietnam, India, and the United States.

Of course, most of us will not start prison ministries or organize airlifts, but we can all support the church's mission of world evangelization through prayer, encouragement, and financial support.

Ministry to the world, however, is not limited to the traditional overseas mission fields. In most cases we no longer have to travel long distances to minister cross-culturally. The world has come to our doorstep. People from various cultures, ethnic groups, and nationalities now live in most of our cities and on most of our university campuses. Never before have we had so many opportunities to minister to the peoples of the world right in our own backyard.

Each of us is surrounded by scores of opportunities to minister—within our churches, to our families, to our communities, and to the world. None of us can say yes to every need. But we can all say yes to those to which God calls us.

Some are called to minister to the church gathered. But most of the church's ministry is to take place when the sanctuary is empty, when the church is scattered.

One church regularly reminded its members of this reality by placing above the sanctuary exit a sign that said "Servants' Entrance." This coming Sunday as you leave your church's sanctuary, remember: You are not leaving the church behind; you are taking the church to the world. You, as a member of the body of Christ, are being sent out to proclaim God's good news by word and deed to a world that desperately needs God's love.

Many laypeople feel that because of their work they have fewer opportunities to minister than do ministry professionals. In fact, most laypeople have an access to people outside the church that most ministry professionals will never have. Being a layperson, far from limiting your opportunities for ministry, actually puts you on the frontlines.

The Myth of Secular Work

Jan Lundy runs a ministry organization, but you won't find it listed in the Yellow Pages under that heading. You'll have to look under "Laboratories." Her business, Precision Histology, is a medical laboratory in Oklahoma City which prepares microscope slides of tissues from which doctors diagnose patients' illnesses.

Precision Histology has been in business for ten years now, and as the world measures success, it has not made much of a splash. For the first few years Jan had to reinvest all her earnings into the company to buy equipment, and today she earns only a modest wage. But that's okay with Jan because Precision Histology is succeeding at what it was created to do.

"From the beginning, our main purpose has been to help people," Jan explains. This happens in various ways. Jan hired lab technicians with little or no technical skill and gave them on-the-job training. Often these were mothers from low-income families who lacked the resources to pay for formal training. One technician she hired was already trained but was recovering from drug addiction and was not physically able to go back to work in the hospital. Jan also made it possible for employees to keep their children with them at work by providing a play area at the lab and, when necessary, hiring a child-care worker at no cost to the mothers.

Karen, one of Jan's first trainees, has recently returned to work for Jan full-time after gaining hospital experience. "Jan gave me a job when I had no job and no training to get a job," she says. "Christy was just six weeks old then, and because Jan made it possible for me to keep Christy with me at work, I was able to nurse her."

Jan relates to her employees not just as individuals but as families, including spouses and children in company social events. And, of course, in all these relationships she tries to show God's love and share her faith in appropriate ways.

As part of its ministry the lab has prepared slides at no charge for three local nonprofit clinics serving low-income patients. But, at its most basic, the lab ministers through the services it is paid to provide. As the name she chose for her company implies, Jan insists upon work of the highest quality, both from herself and her employees. "I treat each slide as though it is for a member of my own family," Jan says. "After all, each one is for *somebody's* mother, brother, or sister."

Once when a lab employee delivered slides to a client, the doctor noticed a problem with one of them. He told the employee, "I know Jan will take care of this, because she's very religious." That doctor recognized that the conscientiousness he had come to expect from Precision Histology was a direct expression of Jan's faith.

"Caring whether people have a good diagnosis is very important to me," says Jan. "Doctors need to be able to interpret slides easily and accurately. If my slides enable them to do that, I am ministering to the patients whether they know it or not." Most of the people to whom Jan and her coworkers minister, then, are people they never meet, but that doesn't make their ministry any less real or important.

Secular or Sacred?

God does not view work the way our culture does. Our culture identifies a few vocations—those involving "professional ministry"—as sacred. Other vocations—such as accountant, sanitation worker, homemaker, and mechanic—it labels secular. These jobs, according to the conventional wisdom, are not concerned with religion.

However, God does not want us to divide life into the religious and nonreligious, the secular and the holy. God calls us to live in a way that makes our entire lives sacred. Paul writes, "So whether you eat or drink or whatever you do, do it all for the glory of God" (1 Cor. 10:31). God calls us to do everything we do, from eating breakfast in the morning to working during the day to playing with our kids in the evening, with the purpose of bringing glory to God—causing others to think more highly of him. For the Christian, every aspect of life, every moment of every day, is to be holy.

Ministering *through* our work means more than simply ministering *while at* work. Many Christians look for appropriate opportunities to talk about their faith with coworkers, clients, or customers. This is important, but ministering through our work goes beyond this. Some people minister by modeling such Christian virtues as honesty, respect, and diligence in workplaces where lying, put-downs, and loafing are the norm. Such integrity can be a powerful witness. But ministering through our work goes still further.

Ministering through our work means ministering to people's needs by the very work we do. Is this possible? Is it possible to minister by the act of baking bread? By the act of typing a letter? By the act of changing a diaper or washing dishes? Is it possible to minister by the act of driving a truck or building a house?

If we understand that ministry isn't restricted to meeting spiritual needs but includes responding in Christian love to any kind of need, the answer is *yes*. You may have been ministering through your work for many years, even if you have not known to call it that.

Does this mean that all workers minister through their work? No, it doesn't. Whether your work is also ministry depends on the kind of work you do, as well as the spirit in which you do it.

Assessing Your Job as Ministry

Test #1: Does Your Work Meet Needs?

In the New Testament the primary word for ministry is *diakonia,* which means "service." If you compare different versions of the New Testament, you will find that the various forms of *diakonia* are often translated "service" and "serve" in one version and "ministry" and "minister" in another, or even both ways within the same version. To minister, then, is to serve. It is to meet another's need.

When Jan Lundy and her employees prepare slides, they are meeting needs. They are helping to diagnose patients' illnesses so that their doctors can prescribe appropriate treatment.

The cashier at your grocery store is helping to provide your family with food—an important need. The auto mechanic who repairs your car meets a need. Because the people doing these jobs meet people's needs, their jobs can be ministries.

Some jobs, though, do not meet people's needs. Manufacturing cigarettes, for example, meets no legitimate need, and the product causes widespread suffering and death. No matter how socially respectable a job may be, if it doesn't help to provide a service or product that meets people's needs, it is not ministry.

Test #2: Do You Have a Servant Spirit?

For a job to be Christian ministry, though, it is not enough that it meet a need. It must also be motivated by servanthood.

When Melody, Eddy's wife, was in the hospital for the birth of their fourth child, she felt surrounded by God's care. This was due in no small part to the ministry of compassionate Christian nurses. One nurse, though, did not want to be there. She came into the room complaining that she had been called in. She complained about which floor she had been assigned to. She performed her duties but never had a pleasant word for the patient. For her, taking care of Melody was not an opportunity to serve; it was just a job. Melody did not feel ministered to by that nurse.

A servant spirit can transform any useful job into a ministry. If a bank's computer programmer approaches the work not just as a way to earn a paycheck or increase the bank's profits but as a way to serve the bank's customers with fast, accurate, dependable service—something we all need—the job can become a ministry, even if the programmer never meets the customers. Being motivated by God's love for others is what makes the difference. Whenever a Christian works with a caring commitment to serve the people to whom he or she is providing needed goods or services, the work itself becomes more than a job; it is transformed into ministry.

The People You Serve

When you work—whether at home, in an office, or in the cab of an eighteen-wheeler—who is it you are serving? Whose needs are you meeting with the product or service you help to provide? If you can answer that question, you are halfway toward having a ministry job rather than a secular job.

To go the other half of the way, you simply have to do your work *for* those people. Your goal, as you work, is to serve them, to meet their needs.

Eddy: I heard of one Christian builder who prays for the family that will live in the home he is building. A quilter prays for the family that will spend cold nights snuggled under her quilt. These workers have found a way to remind themselves of who it is they are serving. They are inspired by the fact that their work will minister to specific people, though they have not yet met. Not only are they lovingly preparing a house and a quilt for future owners, by their prayers they are also releasing God's blessing into the lives of those they serve.

Remembering who it is you are serving can turn ordinary tasks into ministry. One mother we know confesses that initially when her baby demanded to be held, she was tempted to feel as though she were wasting time. As she rocked her baby she wasn't getting lunch prepared; she was not finishing the laundry.

One day, however, as she was impatiently rocking her baby, she remembered the last sentence of a magazine article she had read: "A baby needs to be held when a baby needs to be held." That line reminded her that she was engaged in one of the most important ministries in the world—showing love to her child. She was then able to relax and concentrate on "doing love," confident there was no better way to invest her time.

How can you remind yourself of who it is you're serving with your work? By putting a picture of a representative customer on the wall above your desk? By praying for the person who will receive each package you send out of the shipping room? By offering a warm smile and a kind word to each customer you wait on? Whatever your reminder is, allow a vision of the people you serve through your work to inspire you to add the secret ingredient of love to every task. When love for those you serve inspires your daily work, your work becomes ministry.

No Christian should do "secular" work—work that is not holy or sacred. Every Christian's work, whether paid or unpaid, done at home or the office or the factory, is to be done to glorify God and serve other people.

Beyond the Job Description

Approaching your work with a servant spirit can transform any worthwhile task into ministry. But your work presents you with further opportunities for ministry—opportunities that go beyond your job description.

Mark, the insurance agent you met in chapter 1, has always tried to give his clients reliable, conscientious service. Because he brings a servant spirit to his job, working for the purpose of meeting his clients' needs, he ministers every day by doing what he is paid to do.

After a few years in the business, however, Mark realized he had been overlooking some important opportunities for ministry. He was struck, for example, with how many of his clients called to have their insurance policies changed due to divorce. Some would call to find out how their insurance rates would be affected if they followed through with the divorce they were considering.

Mark began to think about how these people needed a lot more than insurance quotes. They needed new hope for their marriages. So when these people called, he would give them the figures they asked for and then, if it seemed appropriate, express his concern. Sometimes he would say, "I'll be praying for you." To some he would recommend a book or a video that had helped him in his marriage, or he would refer the couple to his church's counseling service.

"I know of three couples whose marriages have been saved because they followed through on what I suggested to them," Mark says.

During the past year Mark has become more intentional about sharing his faith with people he meets through his job. He realizes that however sensitive he may try to be in doing this, he still runs a risk of offending some people and losing their business. "But," Mark says, "I've decided that sometimes I've got to stick my neck out and take that risk.

"Not long ago a man who was going through some hard times called to set up an appointment to talk about his insurance. Because his lifestyle was so obviously different from mine, I thought that if anyone would be offended at my sharing my faith, this guy would. But when I woke up on the morning of our appointment, I sensed the Holy Spirit saying, 'I'm going to give you a chance to talk with him about spiritual things.'

"When I met with him later that day, I did get to tell him how God could help him with his problems. He said, 'I can't believe this. You're the third or fourth person to say that to me this week.' Before he left my office that day, he'd let me pray with him."

What kinds of opportunities for ministry does your work offer you—above and beyond the basic requirements of your job? What spiritual needs do you see in those you encounter through your work? What emotional needs? What needs for practical help? What financial needs? How can you respond to these needs in ways that demonstrate God's love?

The Right Job?

Most of us, as we come to better understand that we are called to minister through our work, will wonder, "Is the job I have the best place for me to live out God's good news, or could I have a greater ministry in some other kind of work?" It is an important question.

When you ask yourself this question, either one of two things is true, according to pastor Gordon Cosby. "Your dissatisfaction is God's instruction to learn to do every task to his glory, or it is God calling you to cast your nets in another place. If it is the first, there will be the contentment of consecrated work; if it is the latter, the dissatisfaction will persist."[13]

What may be the best possible setting for ministry for one person—as the insurance business seems to be for Mark—will not be at all right for another person, with a different personality, interests, and spiritual gifts. While it is not always easy to know what kind of work God is calling us to—or even what role he wants us to take in our churches, families, or communities—it is possible for each of us to learn to recognize God's call. In the next chapter we'll look at how to do just that.

Where do you mourn with Jesus for the pain in the world? What would give you joy in this painful situation?

Where the world's deep pain and your deep joy intersect, there you find your call.

5

Discovering Your Call

"The church has forgotten me. Nobody cares," an elderly shut-in told his pastor. Bob Martin was moved by this man's story when the pastor told it in church the next Sunday. After the service Bob asked his pastor for the man's name and address.

Walter Gooden, Bob learned, was eighty years old. His only family was an older brother, who seldom visited. He had no one in the world who cared about him.

Over the next two years Walter's house became a regular stop for Bob. They sat around and talked a lot, went to the grocery store together, went to doctor's appointments together. When Walter was moved to a nursing home, Bob continued visiting him, and when Walter went to the hospital, Bob was there. Shortly after Bob moved away from Wichita, he was called back to attend Walter's funeral.

After his move to Oklahoma City, Bob had a similar experience with an elderly lady. He went to see her every day and took her lunch on Sundays. After a man beat her and tried to rape her, Bob was there to comfort her.

Bob says, "The Lord used these two experiences to burden my heart for compassionate ministries." Today Bob leads his church's Compassionate Ministries team in reaching out to a growing number of needs like these.

It is important for each of us to discover the ministries God is calling us to. If we try to do a little of everything, we will end up doing nothing well. Just as each part of the human body has certain functions, so God has given each member of the body of Christ specific jobs to do. The only way the body can work as God intends is for each member to do his or her own jobs well.

How can we know what ministries God wants us to do? One pastor advises his members, "If God has burdened you about a particular need in a person's life and you are able to meet that need and minister to that person . . . , then proceed prayerfully and thoughtfully."[14] Bob's first step in discovering his niche in ministry was simply responding to the need of one person for whom God had burdened him. It is only as we reach out to meet needs that our spiritual gifts can emerge and our calls be clarified.

Gifts for Everyone

Knowing what your spiritual gift is can help you to make wiser decisions about ministry. When Paul wrote to the Corinthians and the Romans, he assumed they already knew what their spiritual gifts were, and in his letter to the Romans he gave specific instructions to each person for how to use his or her gift (12:6–8). So Paul saw practical value in Christians knowing what their gifts are.

Sometimes, though, trying to identify our spiritual gifts can be frustrating. The Bible doesn't define all the spiritual gifts; it just lists them. So different scholars have sometimes come up with vastly different definitions. What we end up calling our spiritual gifts may depend on which book we happen to be reading on that subject or which "test" we have just taken to identify those gifts.

However, the lack of agreement on definitions doesn't mean we can't identify our gifts. It only means we should not be too concerned about matching the "correct" label with each person's gift. What really matters is that we clearly identify the special abilities God has given us for ministry.

Bob Martin, for example, identifies his gift this way: "God has gifted me to reach out and touch a hurt." Bob's spiritual gift is probably what the Bible calls "showing mercy" (Rom. 12:8). He may sometimes refer to his gift that way. But he may find it more helpful to call his gift "showing compassion" or "reaching out and touching hurts," and there is no reason he shouldn't use the phrase that describes the gift most clearly for him.

Sometimes spiritual gifts and talents are confused. While both are gifts from God and often work hand in hand, God has given all people talents. Spiritual gifts operate only through believers, those in whom God's Spirit lives.

A talent is a skill, like painting or writing. A spiritual gift is an ability to allow God's Spirit to touch the spirit of another person through you in a particular way.

For example, singing is a talent. Many non-Christians are good singers. But a Christian who ministers through singing is not only using a talent but also exercising a spiritual gift. That gift may be encouragement, teaching, or even prophecy, depending on what effect the ministry has on the spirits of those who hear the music.

While you don't have to identify your spiritual gift before you can minister, knowing what your spiritual gift is can help you make better-informed decisions about where and how to minister. How then can you identify your spiritual gift?

A gift is visible only when it is in action. As you respond in love to those needs for which God is giving you a special concern, as Bob Martin did, your gift will emerge. Different people respond to identical needs in different ways, depending on what gifts God has given them. It is only as you respond in ministry that the special abilities God has given you for ministry become clear.

The Meaning of *Call*

Our spiritual gifts and our calls to ministry are related but different. First Corinthians 12:4–5 says, "There are different kinds of gifts, but the same Spirit. There are different kinds of service, but the same Lord." Just as there are different spiritual gifts, there are different kinds of service or ministries in which we can use those gifts.

The Bible uses the word *call* to describe God's call to salvation that comes to everyone. We have also talked about how all of us are called to be ministers. But in this chapter we are focusing on yet a third meaning of *call,* on God's call to a *particular* ministry or kind of service.

At the burning bush God called Moses to deliver his people from Egyptian slavery. On the Damascus Road, God called Saul to be a witness to the Gentiles. Today God calls some people to pastoral ministry, evangelism, or missionary work. But God's call comes not only to those in professional ministry; it comes to all of us.

Furthermore, it may come not just once but several times during our lives. While some spiritual gifts can be expected to operate for a lifetime, calls to specific kinds of ministry can change. Many of us will be given different missions for different stages of our lives. How can you know what kind of ministry God is calling you to for this period of your life?

Finding Your Niche in Ministry

What Causes You Pain?

Our own pain can point us to what God is calling us to do. In 1991 Dillard Taylor started a ministry called JobNet, a support group for unemployed and underemployed people. Where did he get the idea? After twenty-three years of continuous employment he suddenly found himself out of work and in need of practical support. His own pain sensitized him to the needs of others in similar situations.

God's call may come to us not through our own pain but through the need of another. A medical doctor in Newton, Kansas, aware that many people in his community could not afford health insurance, organized a low-cost clinic. A black pastor in Jackson, Mississippi, in response to the substandard housing in which many people in his community lived, launched a housing-rehabilitation program. You can probably think of ministries in your own community, perhaps even in your own congregation, that have come into being because someone felt the pain of another.

The Church of the Saviour in Washington, D.C., asks two questions to help people clarify their calls. The first: Where do you mourn with Jesus for the pain in the world? Where in your world is the pain you most long to heal? Is it the pain of homelessness? Of latchkey children? Of racism? Are you burdened about teens who are growing up without a strong commitment to God? Or by the woundedness of adults who were abused as children? Is your heart broken by the unhealthy marriages you see? Or do you mourn your church's limited vision for world missions or its failure to include the poor in congregational life? The pain or frustration that most deeply moves your spirit likely points to your call.

What Gives You Joy?

The second question the Church of the Saviour asks is this: What would give you joy in this painful situation? What is the better world you dream of in relation to this problem? Is it a city in which the homeless have decent shelter and food? A neighborhood where different racial groups work together to understand one another and achieve common goals? Is it a community where those with troubled marriages can find support, acceptance, and practical help in healing their relationships?

Frederick Buechner explains it this way:

> The kind of work God usually calls you to is the kind of work (a) that you need most to do and (b) that the world most needs to have done. If you really get a kick out of your work, you've presumably met requirement (a), but if your work is writing TV deodorant commercials, the chances are you've missed requirement (b). On the other hand, if your work is being a doctor in a leper colony, you have probably met requirement (b), but if most of the time you're bored and depressed by it, the chances are you have not only bypassed (a) but probably aren't helping your patients much either. . . .
>
> The place God calls you to is the place where your deep gladness and the world's deep hunger meet.[15]

Another way to determine your call is to ask yourself, "If I had unlimited resources, what would I dream of doing about this pain?" Even if you have identified the pain that calls you, it may not be self-evident how to respond. It is important to take time to hear from God so that, when you do act, you will know you have been sent.

The Call Inward

Eddy: When our family was ministering in the inner city, I had a strong sense of call that gave my work focus and tremendous energy. Melody, my wife, didn't share that sense of call. I often tried to help her identify her call, but my attempts to help only made her feel more frustrated and guilty.

Then Melody went on a spiritual retreat—the same kind of retreat that had so helped me clarify my call. What she told me when she got back was hardly what I had expected. The retreat leader had told Melody she didn't need a call. She recognized that Melody was burned out, emotionally exhausted from trying to minister. What she needed to do was take care of herself. "Once you're well enough," the retreat leader had said, "a call will come."

That was the first time I realized that there are periods in our lives when God calls us to focus not on outward mission but on our own healing. We may need to take time, for example, to grieve, to overcome an addiction, or to recover from the effects of abuse. Healing is hard work and, in its most intense stages, demands most of our energy. During those times, we need to focus on the healing work without feeling guilty that we have little or no energy for outward mission.

God may also call us away from ministry for times of renewal. And, as in the case of Paul, who spent three years in Arabia after his conversion and before beginning his public ministry (Gal. 1:17–18), there may be periods when our focus is not on ministering in the present but on preparing for ministry in the future.

When God calls us inward, we need to obey that call, and we need to support others who are called to work on the renewal, healing, or preparation of their spirits for future ministry. Once the intense inner work is completed, a call to outward ministry will come.

Trying on a Ministry

Discovering your call is seldom a cut-and-dried process. It usually involves experimenting. If an opportunity for ministry comes your way and you don't know whether you have the gifts needed to work at it, you don't have to be sure you will succeed in it before you give it a try. If, after praying about it, you feel drawn to respond to the need, you can "try on" the ministry for a while to test whether it is a good match for you.

When Shirley Posey was asked to teach an adult Sunday school class, she doubted that teaching was the right place for her. She had taught high school English for several years and had not felt satisfied with her performance. But the Sunday school class had been without a teacher for quite a while, and attendance was dropping, so after praying about it, Shirley agreed to give it a try.

To her surprise, Shirley found that she enjoyed studying and preparing the Sunday school lessons. "It was the best thing that ever happened to me. It forced me to study the Word and memorize it. It prepared me for hard things to come in my life." Not only did she enjoy teaching on Sunday mornings, but she also loved being involved in the lives of her class members, "pastoring" them seven days a week. People responded positively to her ministry, and attendance grew.

Through this process, Shirley says, "I discovered teaching was my spiritual gift." If she hadn't been willing to experiment, Shirley might never have found her gift.

How Gifts Are Confirmed

When you "try on a ministry," one of two things happens. If you have a gift in that area, the church body sees the gift operating and affirms it. If you are not gifted in that area, your experiment is still a success because you have learned something about yourself. You can continue "trying on" other ministries until you find one that uses your gifts.

Shirley has been teaching her Sunday school class for twenty years. During that time the class has grown from twenty-four adults to about a hundred. But the clearest evidence that Shirley is where she belongs is not in how many come to hear her teach but in the lives God has touched through her ministry.

Phil and Ann, charter members of the class, describe how Shirley and her husband, James, supported them through their divorce, then nurtured them individually after the divorce and helped them learn to communicate with each other about the real issues in their relationship. Eventually they were able to remarry. Ann says, "We both know that the Holy Spirit used James and Shirley to reach out to us, wrapped his arms around all of us, and drew us back to him and to each other."

Rowena, who joined the class seven years ago, explains what Shirley's ministry has meant to her. "I was not really interested in Sunday school, but I was convinced by a coworker to attend Shirley Posey's class. I saw that the faces of those in her class had such wonderful, peaceful expressions of love. I asked Shirley how I could get what those in her class had. For the next two years she met with me once a week to disciple me. She helped me learn the importance of staying in the Word. I learned how obedience and prayer could change a life. Shirley truly got me moving in the right direction in my spiritual life." These and many other changed lives confirm that Shirley has the gifts needed for her present ministry.

Gifts and call are confirmed in a second way—by the joy experienced by the one who ministers. "This class has given my life meaning," says Shirley. "It gives me something to get up for and look forward to every day. I've gotten tired sometimes and have wanted time off, but I have never wanted to quit."

The Genius of Team Ministry

Many acts of ministry are spontaneous responses to needs we encounter during the day. But obeying a call usually involves a major commitment to a specific kind of ministry over a period of years. None of us alone has all the gifts needed for a major, long-term ministry, but when gifts are blended, new possibilities for ministry are created. When people minister as a team they can support and encourage one another, and work can be shared so that no one is overburdened.

How are ministry teams formed? Some can be formed simply by bringing together people already involved in similar ministries. For example, the director of children's ministries in your church might host monthly meetings for all the children's Sunday school teachers. At these gatherings the director could outline her vision for the church's ministry to children, and teachers could talk about what they feel called to do. Teachers could discuss problems and work out solutions and make programming and curriculum decisions together. They could mention students with special needs and pray for their students and each other.

Ministry teams can be created for any church activity that involves two or more people in ministry—music or visitation, ministry to teens or to senior adults.

Ministry teams can also take the form of support groups for ministries of the church scattered. For example, foster parents in the church could get together regularly to share joys and pains, questions and learnings, and to encourage and pray for one another. They might also work out practical ways to support each other, such as trading off child care to give each other a break. Or a group of business executives might get together weekly over lunch to discuss ways they can transform their jobs into ministries and to hold each other accountable for following through on ministry goals and spiritual disciplines.

Then, of course, a ministry team can be formed to start a new ministry. The Church of the Saviour in Washington, D.C., invites members who believe that God may be giving them a vision for a new ministry to first test the call with church leaders, then to "sound a call" to the rest of the church body. This sounding of a call may take the form of a printed announcement describing the vision or a presentation in a worship service. Others in the congregation are invited to consider whether God is calling them to that same ministry. Whenever two or more people are called to the same ministry, a team is formed.

However we do it, we need to connect with others within our own congregations—and in some cases with people in other congregations—whom God is calling to the same ministry. Only as we work together is the power of body life released into our ministries.

As we respond in compassion to needs God brings across our paths, our gifts become active. As we name our gifts, our ministries take on clearer focus. As we find the point where the world's deep pain and our deep joy intersect, we discover our callings. And as we join with others who share our callings and whose gifts complement ours, we are forged into ministry teams through which God's power and love can flow to heal a hurting world.

As more and more people join together in obeying God's call, the result will be nothing short of a revolution. In fact, as the next chapter shows, the revolution has already begun.

If the average church should suddenly take seriously the notion that every laymember—man or woman—is really a minister of Christ, we could have something like a revolution in a very short time.

Elton Trueblood

6

Joining the Revolution

Revolutions in Progress

A Revolution in California

One Sunday two Cambodian junior high girls rode the Sunday school bus to Long Beach First Church. In the weeks that followed, other Cambodian children joined them. A Sunday school teacher, Letha George, thought, "Here's a people that are sending their children to church, but if I don't do something to get the parents, I'll never keep the children."[16] So she sent letters home with the children inviting their parents to Sunday school.

The next Sunday five women came. A few weeks later men started coming too. When the adult class for Cambodians grew to twenty or twenty-five, Letha wondered, "My goodness, what have I done? These people here at church may run me off!"

However, Long Beach was not that kind of church. Other members volunteered to work with the Southeast Asians, and within months the ministry had mushroomed into three large classes, one each for adults, youth, and children.

John and Mildred Schmidt, a retired couple who had been active in the congregation since 1922, saw how much the Cambodians wanted and needed to learn English. They volunteered to go into the Asian community to teach English as a second language, often using the English Bible as a text. Sometimes, as they took students home after a study session or a social event, John and Mildred had opportunity to lead them to Christ. Many more young people accepted Christ during the actual class sessions.

Church members got involved in many ways, from bus ministry outreach to holding citizenship classes to moving furniture to help with finding jobs. By the time John Calhoun came as senior pastor, over three hundred Cambodians were attending the worship service each week. Glenn and Letha George were leading a large adult Sunday school class and conducting multilingual Sunday morning worship services in the church's fellowship hall. Today some of the Cambodian men testify that they are Christians more because of Glenn's broad smile, warm handshakes, and his arm so often wrapped around their shoulders than because of the preaching of the gospel.

The Asian church kept growing, and it soon became clear that they needed a facility of their own. Though it meant delaying the expansion of their own facility, Long Beach First Church donated their financial reserves to the Cambodians to buy their own building. In February 1986 a building in the heart of the Asian community was dedicated, with nearly 900 people crammed into a sanctuary designed for 450.

This facility is now the meeting place of the two congregations—one speaking the Khmer language and one a Lao dialect—that make up the New Life Church. In addition to hosting six hundred worshipers each week, this building also houses an Asian Bible college extension. Here Southeast

Asians prepare for leadership in ministry, not only among refugees but also in their homelands to which God is leading some to return.

Ung Ty, for example, came to Christ through the outreach of the New Life Church and eventually became pastor of the Khmer congregation. In 1992 he and his wife returned to Cambodia as missionaries. Each week over a thousand people gather to worship at the church he pastors in Phnom Penh. New Life's ministry has also led to the birth of an Asian church in Visalia, California, and both Khmer- and Lao-speaking congregations in Modesto, California.

Long Beach First Church's Asian outreach has brought new life not only to hundreds of Cambodians but also to the parent congregation, especially the lay members who have ministered among the Cambodians week after week. Volunteer Ruth Anderson says, "I had hoped I might find some way to minister to the people of New Life. What I discovered was that their ministry to me gave me *new life*. They have shown me a love I've rarely experienced."

A Revolution in Oklahoma

In 1989 the First Church in Bethany, Oklahoma, was in the midst of what they called a Fifty Day Spiritual Adventure leading up to Easter. During this time the pastor's sermons all focused on bringing Christ's hope to the surrounding community. Hundreds of members committed themselves to five spiritual disciplines, including keeping a spiritual journal and reading the Christian classic *In His Steps,* by Charles M. Sheldon. As members began taking seriously the question posed by the book—"What would Jesus do?"—it became clear that the Holy Spirit was performing something special in many of their lives.

"We knew it wouldn't be right to just end the fifty days, then return to church as usual," said Dave McKellips, associate pastor. "People were being renewed, revived, and they needed to respond." The church provided a way.

At the end of the fifty days members were asked to name needs they saw in the community to which they felt God might want the church to reach out. Suggestions were sorted into thirteen areas. Then one Sunday a bulletin insert listed these thirteen areas of potential ministry and extended the following invitation: "Look over the list of ministry groups, find the one that most interests you, and go to the corresponding room at 5:00 P.M. tonight."

The insert listed four community ministries already in progress—a ministry to the elderly, a prison ministry, a Meals-on-Wheels program, and a ministry with the chemically-dependent and their families. It also listed nine possible new ministries that had been suggested by members, including ministries with the hearing-impaired, the hungry and homeless, and adults who needed tutoring. The insert explained that a new Community Ministry Group would be started for each area in which four or more people were willing to get involved.

Lay ministry is nothing new at Bethany First Church. The congregation has a long history of strong and distinguished lay leadership. But the Holy Spirit was up to something new that spring, and people were offered a new way to respond. Rather than new ministries having to be approved by various committees and boards and then operated under their direction, laypeople were turned loose to start grassroots groups. While church staff would eagerly encourage and support these ministries, ownership and leadership would rest with those to whom God had given the specific vision and calling.

The pastoral staff also made clear that every group had permission to fail. Groups did not have to wait until they had so many volunteers and resources that they felt assured of success before they started. In fact, it was to be expected that, though some groups would develop long-term ministries, others would experiment with a new outreach for a while, only to discover that they did not have the right combination of resources to make it work. And that was okay.

With this freedom to take risks, the people of Bethany First Church began to dream new dreams and experiment with new ministries. Some of those original Community Ministry Groups are still going strong today. Others have dissolved. Yet others have arisen as God continues to plant vision in the hearts of people throughout the congregation. Excerpts from the church's newsletter for its Community Ministries highlight the varied ways people are touching their community with God's love.

Ten months ago the Bethany First Church RAIN (Regional AIDS Interfaith Network) Team was assigned their first client. We were not sure how we were going to react to Mike or how he was going to react to us, but we were committed to represent the love of Jesus to this young man during the final stages of his life.

Last week we, as a team, attended Mike's funeral. Mike had become a friend to all of us. We were given not only the opportunity to serve Mike in a variety of ways, but also the special privilege of walking hand in hand with him to death's door. I believe all of us on the RAIN team would readily admit that we received much more than we gave during the ten months we cared for Mike.

Linda Shaw has been heading up a wonderful ministry at Mabel Bassett [a women's prison] for the past two years. Between 20 and 25 women regularly attend the Bible study.

Another group holds regular worship services at various correctional institutions [for men] around the state and have done so for several years. If you are interested in joining them, contact Lloyd Keith.

Two years ago I began to look for ways I could contribute to our compassionate ministries program. A black sign-up book for Meals-on-Wheels was passed around our Sunday school class. This seemed like a way to help without having to find a babysitter for my two children. The three of us set out only to deliver meals to the elderly, but came home with a book of poetry, homemade bread, and more hugs than we could count.

Volunteer teams are forming to renovate the two remaining apartment units at Bethlehem Transitional Shelter for Homeless Families. Bob Martin has volunteered to serve as coordinator. Volunteers are not required to have any special skills or tools.

Looking for a different Friday night experience? Every fifth Friday (four times a year) we [go to] the City Rescue Mission. We have lots of singing and a short message from the Bible. There are always people to pray with. If the joy of service isn't enough, we always go out for pizza afterward!

Senior pastor Melvin McCullough identifies two lessons he learned from the renewal at Bethany First Church that gave birth to many of these ministries: "First, I learned that in spiritual renewal the Holy Spirit can use not only an anointed evangelist or concerned pastor who has a vision for revival, but can use perhaps even more powerfully the personal testimonies of laypeople who have been genuinely revitalized.

"Second, the hundreds of people who received new spiritual energy recognized immediately that they needed an outlet for service and social action that would penetrate the community around us. It has been one of the most meaningful experiences of my pastoral ministry to observe a spiritual awakening that bears such observable fruit in transforming the culture and the community."

A Revolution in Ontario

In 1989 a church in Brampton, Ontario, redefined Pastor Reg Graves's job description, directing him to focus his time and energy in three areas: preaching, crisis visitation, and supporting the ministry of several lay pastors whom he would appoint, subject to board approval. All his other responsibilities would be assigned to lay pastors and teams of laypeople who would work with them.

Brampton now has seven lay pastors, each responsible for one area of the church's life—stewardship, small groups, missions, children's ministries, outreach, visitation, music, or prayer. A ninth area, youth ministry, was led by lay pastors until it became necessary to hire a full-time youth pastor.

As new people come into the congregation, they are invited to participate in a class, offered three times a year, on discovering their spiritual gifts. They are then encouraged to become involved in one of the congregation's nine areas of ministry.

Members are clear about where the responsibilities for ministry lie. When a problem arises in children's ministries, for example, it is not taken to Pastor Graves but to the lay pastor for children's ministries. And the pastor no longer attends so many committee meetings. Finance committee meetings, for example, are handled by the lay pastor for stewardship.

Since the first lay pastor was appointed five years ago, the church has grown from 160 to 250. To minister to the needs of the growing congregation, more lay pastors are appointed as needed.

How does Pastor Graves feel about his new role? "I admit that some things have been difficult for me to give up," he says, "but, overall, these years have been the most rewarding I've ever had as a pastor. I've been freed up to do the things I do best and enjoy the most."

Not only has Pastor Graves been freed to concentrate on what he does best, but laypeople have been empowered to minister as never before, and more and more lives are being touched by God's love through the congregation.

A Revolution in Kansas

When Newton First Church offered a class on lay ministry, Rick Brenneman was intrigued by his pastor's excitement about the class and so signed up. "I went into the class thinking our pastor's job was to do ministry for us," Rick says. "I came away from the class understanding that our pastor's job is to equip us to go out and minister."

One of the first places this made a difference for Rick was on his job at a funeral home. "What I do at work has changed very little," Rick explains, "but my attitude has changed. Going to work used to be just a duty, a responsibility. It's still a responsibility, but now when I leave home in the morning, I'm not just going to work; I'm going to a ministry. This attitude gives me a new reason for going to work and new energy for my job, and the way I relate to people is more caring."

Before the class, Rick was serving the church as an usher and a member of the board. Learning how to identify his gifts and calling helped Rick realize that these duties had come to feel like a burden to him and that perhaps these were not the places where God wanted him to be serving.

His new role in the church is to periodically teach a class on lay ministry—the same class he had attended earlier—and to lead a support group for class graduates who are working to clarify their calls or starting new ministries. Rick finds energy and joy in his new ministry as he sees people intentionally moving into ministry for the first time in their lives.

One support-group member, for example, felt she had no ministry to offer. Rick knew, though, that she was gifted at making handcrafts. Another member had already begun a ministry of visiting nursing homes. "What if you made crafts as gifts for the nursing home residents, and Vern could deliver them when he visits the nursing home?" Rick suggested. And so two group members began cooperating and reached out in a way that neither of them could have done alone.

One couple in the group, Ford and Dot Burkhart, became responsible during a very short time for the care of four elderly relatives. "Because of what we learned in this class, we are absolutely convinced that caring for these elderly loved ones is a ministry," Dot says. "If we did not see it that way, it could be a real drudgery. Taking over the power of attorney involves a lot of paperwork as well as a lot of emotional support, and sometimes it can seem like a thankless job. But now we see this as an opportunity from God."

Norman Rogers, another graduate of the lay ministry class, has launched what he calls the Muscle Ministry. Twelve to fifteen men in the congregation have volunteered to be on call for needs that require muscle power. When someone in the church reports a need, Norman contacts the crew and they go to work. The Muscle Ministry group has done heavy yard work for elderly members, such as removing trees and shrubs; they have cleaned storm drains and helped people move, as well as doing a little work on the church grounds.

The entire church has a greater consciousness about ministry. People can be overheard saying, "Thank you for your ministry," in response to an act as simple as making coffee for a Sunday school class. It is not uncommon for members in casual conversation to say lightheartedly, "Well, there's a ministry!" And quite a few members are going into their workplaces with a new attitude and a new sense of mission as they have come to see their jobs not as just jobs but as ministries.

Christ's Hands in a Broken World

If the church is to fulfill its mission in this time of soaring need, we laypeople cannot sit back and leave ministry to the professionals. We must say yes to God's call and join with our pastors and other leaders in forming a dynamic partnership in ministry.

During World War II a statue of Christ that stood at the center of a small French village was shattered in the fighting. Villagers carefully saved the pieces until the war was over, then rebuilt the statue. Once it had been reassembled, though, the people found that Christ's hands were missing. They weren't sure what to do. Should they leave the incomplete statue up, or should they take it down? Only when someone placed a small hand-painted sign at the statue's base were the villagers able to agree that the statue was, in fact, complete and should remain. The sign read, "Christ has no hands but ours."

Are you willing to commit the rest of your life to being Christ's hands in a broken world? God wants to use you—not someday but right now. God wants to use you—not sometime but all the time. God wants to use you—not somewhere but right where you are.

After all, ministry isn't just for "ministers." On second thought, though, ministry *is* just for ministers, for God has called you and me and every other believer to be his ministers and entrusted us with his mission. If we do not accept the task, no one will. Christ has no hands but ours. Will you join the revolution?

Study/Action Guide

How to Use This Guide

A Note to Pastors and Lay Leaders

If you dream of mobilizing and equipping all the people of your congregation for ministry, this book was written with you and your people in mind. While we hope the book will help all who read it, we believe it will have its greatest impact when used for its primary purpose—as a tool to stimulate congregational renewal. If as many as 20 percent of the adults in your church complete this study and then act on what they have learned, it could well prove to be a watershed event in your congregation's history.

This study/action guide gives detailed, activity-by-activity instructions for six sessions, each forty-five minutes to an hour long. Sessions include discussion, reading of Scripture and stories, and sharing and prayer in small groups, but no lectures. Because the lesson plans are so complete, the leader should need to spend only an hour or so preparing for each session.

Finding a Setting

This course lends itself to various settings. It can be a congregation-wide study held during six consecutive Wednesday or Sunday evening services. One church offered it as an optional class before the Sunday evening service. Another church held a churchwide study of lay ministry as a creative alternative to their usual fall revival, meeting each weeknight for a week and climaxing on Sunday morning. Or you might organize an all-church weekend retreat around this study.

It can also be used with smaller groups. You could offer the class as an adult Sunday school elective. Existing small groups might study this course in their regular meetings. It could even be used as the basis for a church leadership retreat for board members and their spouses.

Most who complete this study will emerge from it with a broader understanding of ministry and greater vision for the future of the church. So the more who participate in the study, the greater the likelihood that a "critical mass" of laypeople will become catalysts for creating a new level of consciousness about ministry throughout the congregation.

Choosing the Teacher

A member of the pastoral staff may want to lead this study to demonstrate strong commitment to each layperson's ministry. On the other hand, having a layperson lead the study will model lay ministry. One good option might be for a church staff member and a layperson to teach the class together, demonstrating staff support and modeling not only lay leadership but partnership in ministry as well.

More important than whether the study leader is a staff member or layperson are the skills of the teacher. Look for a teacher who knows how to lead lively class discussions. Do not choose a teacher who tends toward a lecture style. The ability to lecture well is a wonderful gift but is not needed or appropriate for this study.

Adapting the Study to Your Needs

These sessions have been thoroughly field-tested in a local church to make sure they really work. While we hope you find the instructions helpful, do not feel limited by them. For example, if a session suggests more activities than you have time for, simply select those activities you feel will be most valuable. Feel free to add, drop, or modify activities as needed to make the sessions work well for your group.

Using the Text

Each person or couple in your group should have a copy of this book. The book will often be used in class, and it is hoped that each participant will read every chapter in full at home. No session, however, depends on participants' reading the chapter before class. In fact, this study/action guide is unusual in that each session is intended to *introduce* a chapter, not to build on the participants' study of it. That means that at your first meeting, for example, you will distribute copies of the book, lead your group through session 1, and *then* suggest that the participants read chapter 1 when they get home. The idea is to so intrigue your group members with the session's topic that they will want to learn more when they leave the session. Because of this structure, visitors to your sessions should be able to participate fully in all activities.

Moving from Study to Action

Since the study's purpose is to mobilize the members of your church for ministry, the course will be a failure if people merely come, learn, enjoy, then go on as they always have.

How can the church support those who are ready to move out in new ministry initiatives? How can those already involved in ministry be brought together in teams?

A member of the pastoral staff should closely monitor the progress of the class and be prepared to propose specific ways participants can implement what they have learned about ministry and their own calls. This may involve creating new structures for team ministry. (See the last two sections of chapter 5 and sessions 5 and 6 of the study/action guide.) It may mean organizing a continuing support group in which members can encourage one another as they work at identifying their calls and trying on new ministries. Unless people have practical ways to translate into action what they've learned, the study will likely be a wasted effort. But if it is used as a springboard to launch people into greater ministry, it may prove to be a turning point for the congregation.

The Ministry Myth

Session goal: To enable each believer present to recognize and affirm that God has called him or her to be a minister.

Materials and advance preparation needed:

1. Paper and pencil for each participant
2. Chalkboard or newsprint and marker
3. Before the session, ask two people to be prepared to read from chapter 1—one to read Gary's story (from the beginning of the chapter up to the first subhead) and one to read Mark's (which begins with the second paragraph under "The High Cost of the Myth").
4. Bibles

Activity 1

Expectations from This Study (5–10 min.)

If the members of this group have come together specifically to explore lay ministry, a good place to begin is to invite each person present to tell why he or she has come. Some may have come just out of curiosity, but most probably have specific hopes or felt needs that have brought them to the session. You will want to listen carefully to what people are hoping to receive from this study, so that in the coming weeks you can emphasize the aspects of the study that speak to their concerns.

If you are using this as curriculum in a Sunday school class or some other existing group, "Why are you here?" may not be the best question to begin with. Ask instead: *What would you like to get out of this study?*

If not all group members know each other, each member should give his or her name before answering the question.

Activity 2

Ministry Is . . . (5–10 min.)

Pass out blank paper and a pencil to each person. Say: *Do you remember the cartoons that would start out "Love is . . ." and would then be followed by a description of love and a drawing to illustrate it? We are going to do the same thing, but with the concept of ministry. The important thing here is not to produce impressive artwork; this is just an activity to help us start thinking about ministry. So across the top of your paper, write: "Ministry is. . . ." Across the bottom of your paper, finish that sentence; then draw a cartoon to illustrate your definition of ministry.*

Allow a minute or so for people to work; then ask them to share responses. Write their answers on a chalkboard or newsprint that says at the top, "Ministry is. . . ."

Activity 3

The Ministry Myth (10–15 min.)

Say: *Having a clear and biblical understanding of the nature of ministry is important, because misconceptions can cause confusion or even paralysis in our spiritual lives. I have asked a couple group members to read stories of people who paid a high price because they believed mistaken ideas about ministry.*

The two people you have recruited before class will now read Gary's and Mark's stories from chapter 1. After the stories are read, say: *Most of us have been frustrated about ministry at some time. Your frustrations may be similar to Mark's or Gary's, or they may be different. What frustrations do you experience in relation to ministry?*

Once again, listen carefully for clues about what you'll need to emphasize in the coming weeks.

Activity 4

Who Are the Ministers? (8–10 min.)

Ask for five volunteers to read the following passages of Scripture: 1 Peter 4:10–11; Romans 12:6–8; 1 Corinthians 12:4–7; 1 Peter 2:5, 9; Revelation 1:6. After the reading of the first three passages, ask the following questions:

1. *To whom does the Holy Spirit give spiritual gifts?* (All believers.)
2. *What is the purpose of spiritual gifts?* Various answers are correct. The point you want to bring out is that they are gifts for ministry.
3. *Then who are the ministers?* (All believers.)

Before the reading of the last two passages of Scripture, ask the group members to listen for the key word that these verses have in common. Once the verses have been read, ask:

1. *What key word do these verses have in common?* (Priest.)

2. *In the Old Testament, who were priests?* (The Levites.) The point to be made here is that it was only a select group. Not all people of faith were priests.

3. *According to these verses, who are priests today?* (All believers.) Explain briefly what it means to be a priest (see chapter 1).

Next, read Ephesians 4:11–12a from the Revised Standard Version or New Revised Standard Version. The reason for using one of these versions is that they use the word *ministry*. Some other versions use the word *service*. If group members compare, you can point out that *service* and *ministry* are different translations of the same Greek word.

After reading this passage, ask:

1. *According to this passage, why has God called certain people to roles of leadership in the church?* (To equip the saints for the work of ministry.)

2. *Who then are the ministers?* (All the saints, or all God's people.)

3. *Which group is to assist the other with ministry? Are the members called to assist the leaders with the ministry of the church, or are the leaders called to help the members with their ministries?* (Leaders are called to equip the members with their ministries.) Optional follow-up question: *Have we sometimes gotten this backward in our thinking?*

4. *So how many of us here are called to be ministers?* You might even ask for a show of hands. It might be good for some people who have never before called themselves ministers to raise their hands.

Activity 5

Ministries in Progress (4–8 min.)

This activity is optional, depending on the time available. If you are left with only ten minutes or so, skip this section and move on to activity 6.

Say: *We have determined that all of us are called to be ministers; actually, most of us are already involved in ministry every day, even if we have never referred to our daily activities as ministries. What are you regularly involved in that you would consider ministry?* Likely answers: ministry to family members, opportunities to express God's love at work or school, etc.

Activity 6

Praying for One Another (8–10 min.)

Form groups of three or four. Suggest that each person in the group share what he or she wants God to do in his or her life during this study; then, in closing, ask the group members to pray for one another.

Reflecting and Looking Ahead

Do you feel that by the end of the session each participant was willing to claim that he or she has been called to minister? If so, you achieved the goal of this session. If not, it doesn't mean that you failed. Some people may take longer than others.

The priesthood of all believers was probably a familiar concept for many of your group members, but the session may have still been significant for them as they shared their ideas about ministry, their frustrations, and what they hope God will do for them in the coming weeks. Did you sense a growing excitement and anticipation about what God is wanting to do in the group and in your church?

Were misconceptions about ministry expressed? Frustrations? Hopes? Keep these in mind as you prepare for future sessions.

Washing Dirty Feet

Session goal: To help each participant realize that God calls us to minister to all kinds of needs, not just spiritual needs.

Materials and advance preparation needed:

1. Chalkboard or newsprint and marker
2. Bibles

Activity 1

Do I Really Have a Ministry? (5 min.)

Say: *One person who enrolled in a group study of lay ministry gave this reason for wanting to explore the topic further: "I have not been effective as a soul-winner, and that leaves me wondering if I really have a ministry." Have any of you ever had similar feelings?*

You might expand the statement to include other activities widely recognized as ministry because they address spiritual needs—teaching, preaching, counseling, leading worship, and so on. The goal of this activity is to encourage group members to express the frustrations they have experienced as a result of feeling that ministry is limited primarily to meeting spiritual needs.

Activity 2

Two Motivations for Ministry (10–20 min.)

Ask for a volunteer to read the story in chapter 2 under the heading "What Needs?" After the story is read, write the following heading and column headings across the top of your chalkboard or newsprint:

Ministry Motivated By

Law	Love

Ask the group: *List some adjectives you would use to describe ministry motivated by law.* Likely answers: judgmental, self-righteous, conditional, guilt-motivated, fear-motivated, etc.

Then ask: *List some adjectives to describe ministry motivated by love.* Likely answers: unconditional, sensitive, accepting, etc.

As group members answer, invite them to explain briefly. Without putting anyone on the spot, give opportunity for people's comments to expand into describing their own experiences. Group members have likely had similar experience in struggling with legalistic motivations for ministry, and it can be healing and empowering for them to discover that they are on the same spiritual journey.

In summary, point out the relationship between love and ministry to the whole person. While law-motivated ministry can be narrowly defined and specify what needs we are obligated to respond to, it is the nature of love to respond to all kinds of needs, not to address spiritual needs and ignore all other kinds of needs.

Activity 3

The Needs Love Touches (10–12 min.)

Ask for four volunteers to read the passages of Scripture cited below. As outlined, briefly introduce the reading of each passage, and follow each reading with the respective questions.

1. *This passage in Luke 4 is sometimes called Jesus' "inaugural address" because he made this statement at the beginning of his public ministry as an announcement of his mission.* (Read Luke 4:14–21.)
What kinds of needs did Jesus say God's Spirit had sent him to meet?

2. *Toward the end of Jesus' ministry John the Baptist sent two of his disciples to Jesus to ask whether he was, in fact, the Messiah. Rather than answer yes or no, Jesus listed certain of his activities, implying that they proved he was the Messiah.* (Read Matthew 11:2–5.)
What kinds of ministry did Jesus feel demonstrated his messiahship? What kinds of needs had he met? Were spiritual needs the only ones he listed?

3. *Jesus may have told this following parable just to make sure there was no room for doubt among his listeners that we too are to minister to the whole person, just as he did.* (Read Matthew 25:31–46.)
Did Jesus make meeting nonspiritual needs optional for his followers, or does he expect this kind of ministry from every one of us?

4. *Finally, one more reminder that love cannot say yes to spiritual needs but no to other kinds of needs.* (Read 1 John 3:17.)
So if we minister to spiritual needs but not to other needs, are we carrying out Christ's mission? If we minister to social

needs but not to spiritual needs, are we carrying out Christ's mission? (No, faithfulness to Christ's mission demands that we respond compassionately to the needs of the total person, both spiritual and social.)

Activity 4

Love in Action (5–8 min.)

Ask one or two volunteers to read the story of Steve and Cyndi Lamb from chapter 2, under the subheading "Behold, How They Love." Or if you know of a similar story that has taken place in your church or community, invite a group member to share that story with the group. An important element in the Lamb story is that the church's outpouring of compassion led to evangelism simply because someone was so impressed at seeing such love in action that she was motivated to investigate what was behind it. If you use a story from your own community, it would be good to choose one that also shows how ministry to nonspiritual needs can result in spiritual needs being met.

Activity 5

A Liberating Call (6–8 min.)

As preparation for this activity, study the section of chapter 2 under the subheading "A Liberating Call." Be prepared to present the content of this section in a three- to four-minute minilecture. After explaining the concepts, say:

1. *Think back to the story of the Lambs* (or the alternative story). *What were some of the different gifts or abilities that people used in ministering to this family?*

2. Did all of these gifts or abilities minister directly to spiritual needs? How might this story have unfolded differently if the only needs ministered to had been the Lambs' spiritual needs? (Or the spiritual needs of the person/people in your alternative story.)

The point, of course, is that for the world to see God's love fully expressed we must respond in love to the needs of the whole person, and when we do, people will take notice.

Write the word *ministry* across the top of your chalkboard or newsprint; then draw a wheel with six or eight spokes. Label one spoke "spiritual needs." Explain: *One reason some people find it so difficult to find their niche in ministry is that they have gotten the idea that this* (point to the "spiritual needs" spoke) *is all there is to ministry. If their particular gifts for ministry don't fit here, they get frustrated and conclude that they don't have a role in ministry. In reality, the problem is that their niche in ministry lies in one or more of these other areas, but they don't know that these areas involve ministry just as much as spiritual needs do.* Label the other spokes with such phrases as "financial needs," "practical needs," "emotional needs."

Everyone here has a God-given ability to minister to one or more of these kinds of needs, and each of your ministries is needed if the church is to fulfill all of Christ's mission in our community.

Activity 6

Washing Feet—Past and Future (5–10 min.)

Form groups of three or four, and ask each person to share with the group (1) one way God has used him or her to meet a need in another person's life and (2) one way he or she will try to "wash dirty feet" during the coming week. This could be anything from volunteering at a food pantry to visiting patients in a nursing home to writing a note of encouragement. The following week each person should come prepared to report on the "foot washing" experience. After all have shared, have the small groups close the session by praying for one another's ministries.

Reflecting and Looking Ahead

Did your group include some with a spiritual-needs-only (or -primarily) view of ministry? If so, has this view caused them any frustration?

Did group members see how love inevitably leads to whole-person ministry? Were they able to visualize whole-person ministry?

If you had some people in your group with the spiritual-needs-only view, did they find the concept of whole-person ministry threatening or liberating? Were any able to identify other areas where they might have ministry gifts? How easy or difficult was it for people to name ways God had used them in other people's lives?

Were any concerns expressed in this session that you think deserve particular attention in the coming weeks?

Session **3**

The Empty Sanctuary

Session goal: To help participants realize that most ministry takes place not when the church is gathered but when the church is scattered; to make them more aware of ways they are ministering or could be ministering when the church is scattered.

Materials and advance preparation needed:

1. Chalkboard or newsprint and marker
2. Paper and pencil for each participant
3. Bibles

Activity 1

A Survey of Ministries (8–12 min.)

Ask your group: *What are some of the ministries of our congregation?*

As answers are called out, list them on a chalkboard or newsprint. Continue for five or six minutes, or until the answers stop coming, whichever comes first. Affirm the importance of all these ministries, and note their number and variety.

Next, lead the group through their list and ask them to indicate which of the ministries take place when the church is gathered (mark these with the letter *G*) and which take place when the church is scattered (mark these *S*). For example, worship services would be marked *G*, and nursing home visitation would be marked *S*. Any ministries that take place in both settings can be marked *GS*.

When the group has gone through the whole list, ask whether there are more Gs or more Ss. If your group has listed more Gs, say: *When we think about the ministries of our congregation, it is easiest to think of the ministries of the church gathered. They tend to be the most visible. But, in reality, most of the ministry of this congregation takes place during the week, when the congregation is scattered.* Go on to give examples of ways that members of the congregation minister through the week—parents ministering to their children, spouses ministering to each other, nurses ministering to their patients, teachers meeting the needs of their students, people doing volunteer work with community organizations, etc. (Read, in advance, chapters 3 and 4 for possible examples.)

Point out that sometimes we think of the church primarily as an organization, so we include only official ministry programs when we list the ministries of the church. But since the church is a body of believers, the ministries of the church include the ministries of all the members of that body. And most of this ministry takes place not when the church is gathered but when the church is scattered.

Why is this important? Because so long as we think of ministry as something that takes place only "at the church" or through a church program, we will fail to recognize that much of what we are doing every day is, or can be, ministry. This misconception can even keep people from discovering their calls. Because they do not recognize that certain activities can be ministry, they may not realize that a desire to serve in such ways is actually a God-given call to ministry.

Activity 2

Purpose of the Church Gathered (6–8 min.)

Ask for a volunteer to read the section of chapter 3 headed "Purpose of the Church Gathered." Then say: *The church gathers for a number of reasons. What are some of those reasons?* Affirm the answers people give. Note that some of the reasons we gather, such as worshiping God, are ends in themselves. We don't do them as a means to do something else. Being a community can have value in and of itself. In these areas the church is different from the sales team described in the passage just read.

However, the church is similar to the sales team in the area of mission. Continue to ask questions, and invite response until you feel that the group has grasped the meaning of the sales team analogy—that a major reason the church gathers is to prepare and equip for its ministry as the church scattered. If the church's gathering does not result in effective ministry of the church scattered during the week, our gathering has failed to meet one of its major purposes.

Activity 3

Where Ministry Happens (6–8 min.)

Ask for a volunteer to read Romans 12:4–8 and to pause each time he or she comes to the name of one of the spiritual gifts, allowing you time to write the name of the gift on your chalkboard or newsprint. Make your list in a column on the left side. Then next to your list make a chart as shown.

	Church gathered	Church scattered
Prophesying		
Serving		
Teaching		
Encouraging		
Giving		
Leadership		
Showing mercy		

Go through the list, gift by gift. Talk briefly about what each gift is. (Don't get hung up on precise definitions; the Bible doesn't define the gifts precisely.) Then ask: *Is this a gift that is exercised when the church is gathered or when the church is scattered?* Put an *X* in the appropriate space. Most, probably all, of the gifts can be exercised in either setting, with a group or one-on-one. If the gift can be used in both but is used more in the one setting than in the other (for example, prophesying is usually done in a group; showing mercy, usually one-on-one), circle the *X* in that column.

This activity has two purposes. The first is to reinforce the idea that ministry takes place just as truly when the church is scattered as when it is gathered. Second, and you will need to point this out, this activity shows that some people's gifts are most often used one-on-one, not in groups. If they think of ministry mainly in terms of gatherings, they may have trouble finding their spiritual gifts or feel they are not gifted. Therefore, when someone is trying to identify his or her call, it is crucial to consider the ministries of the church scattered.

Activity 4

From Sanctuary to Tavern (6–8 min.)

Read (or call on one of your better readers to do so) the Jim Couchenour story found at the beginning of chapter 3. Then say: *Jim had been a deeply committed member of his church for twenty-eight years yet had been unaware of the tremendous human need in the community right around the church. Is it possible that we in our church may have overlooked some of the most pressing human needs right in our own community?*

Activity 5

Opportunities for Ministry (2–6 min.)

Pass out paper and a pencil to each person. Ask your group members to turn their papers so that the long side is up and make four columns. They should label these columns "World," "Community," "Family," and "Church" and draw a line just under these headings. Then ask them to turn their papers so that those headings are on the left edge of the paper, and to draw a line dividing the paper into two vertical columns. Have them head the left column "Needs." For now, leave the second column blank. The chart should look like the one below.

	Needs	
Church		
Family		
Community		
World		

Give the group members two minutes to list needs they are aware of in each of the four categories—church, family, community, world. These can include both needs to which they are ministering and needs to which they are not ministering.

After two minutes, have the group members add the heading "Possible Responses" to the second column, then take a couple minutes to reflect on how they might respond to some of these needs if they felt so led.

If time is running short, skip the chart-making and simply ask the participants to think of (1) one way they are regularly ministering to a need in their church, family, community, or world and (2) one need that they feel God may be wanting them to respond to. They will be asked to share these in the next activity. Try to save at least six minutes for the final activity.

Activity 6

Considering Our Responses (6–10 min.)

Form groups of three or four, and give the following instructions: *Begin by reporting briefly on the act of foot-washing you committed yourself to at the end of the last session. What did you do? How did it go?*

After that, name one need—from your list in the last activity—to which you are already regularly ministering. Then name one need to which you feel God may be wanting you to respond. Once everyone has shared, close by praying for one another, both about your continuing ministries and for guidance regarding future ministries.

Reflecting and Looking Ahead

Each session so far has expanded the definition of ministry. Are your group members seeing that ministry is something every Christian does? That it can be in response to any kind of need? And that it can happen in any setting? Are they beginning to see that most ministry is not organizationally related to the church but happens wherever Christians respond in love to anyone?

These are all simple concepts, but for people to whom they are new they can be life-changing. The next session will focus on how "ordinary" work can be transformed into ministry.

The Myth of Secular Work

Session goal: To help participants understand the relationship between work and ministry and learn how they can minister more effectively through their work.

Materials and advance preparation needed:

1. Tools representing various kinds of work, such as a hammer, overalls, a dish towel, a Bible commentary. Before the session, arrange these in a display at the front of the room.
2. Chalkboard or newsprint and marker
3. Bibles, including several each of the King James Version and contemporary translations

Activity 1

Secular Jobs (3–4 min.)

Open your session something like this: *Today we are going to be talking about ministering through our work. We will not be talking primarily about ministry professionals—like church staff or employees of Christian ministry organizations—though they too may learn something useful from this session. Rather, we are going to be talking about how those of us who work in schools, homes, offices, stores, or factories can minister through our jobs.*

How many here regularly do some kind of secular work— either paid or unpaid? Would you raise your hands?

Okay. Since so many of you do secular work, it should not be too hard for us to come up with a definition of the word secular. *What does* secular *mean?* Optional: Jot answers on a chalkboard or newsprint.

Since most dictionaries define *secular* by saying what it is not (for example, "not religious or related to the church"), you will probably want to ask: *What words are opposites of* secular? Possible answers: religious, sacred, holy.

Activity 2

Ministry Tools (1–2 min.)

Draw attention to the tools you have displayed at the front of the room. Ask: *Which of these are ministry tools? Why?* Don't try to reach a consensus or guide people to the right answer just yet. The purpose of this activity is simply to define the question. The next activity will move you toward an answer.

Activity 3

Transforming "Secular" Jobs (8–10 min.)

Continue by saying: *Most of us (except perhaps those who "cheated" and read the chapter before class) see ourselves as working in secular jobs. Our jobs do not seem particularly religious, holy, or sacred. But it does not have to be that way. In some cases, all that is necessary for us to see our jobs as ministries is to take a new look at what we are already doing. Some of us may need to approach our work in new ways to turn our jobs into ministries. A few may even need to consider changing jobs—if they determine that God cannot be glorified through their present jobs. But every Christian can minister through his or her work, just as truly as the person on the staff of a church or a Christian ministry organization.*

Jan Lundy's story is an example of how a job that is usually considered secular can be approached as a ministry. Ask for a volunteer to read the Jan Lundy story, found at the beginning of chapter 4. After the story is read, ask the group to list the ways Jan ministers through Precision Histology. List their answers on your chalkboard or newsprint.

Once the list is complete, ask the following questions:

1. *Which of these ministries is Jan able to perform because she manages her own business and can therefore set policy?* As people indicate items from the list, mark them with the letter *M,* for "manager." Possible answers: offer employment and job training to those with limited economic opportunities; provide on-site child care to employees, meeting an economic need and strengthening family relationships; including employees' families in social events; preparing slides without charge for nonprofit clinics.

2. *Which of these ministries could she do even if she had no policy-making authority?* Mark these with an *E* to indicate that every "employee" can do these. Possible answers: show God's love and share her faith with coworkers; consistently do work of the highest quality.

3. *What does our analysis suggest about the ministry potential of the owner/manager of a business?* (Such a person is in a position to build the business completely on biblical principles and to base all company policies on the goal of making the entire business a ministry.)

4. *What does our analysis say about the possibility of ministering as an employee?* (Even people who have little or no authority to influence company policies can approach their jobs as ministries.)

Activity 4

Secular or Sacred? (6–10 min.)

Ask for a volunteer to read 1 Corinthians 10:31. Ask for another volunteer to read the section of chapter 4 headed "Secular or Sacred?" Then say: *The key to understanding how our everyday work can also be ministry is found in understanding the basic nature of ministry. In earlier chapters ministry was defined as "doing love" and "loving people as Jesus would." Those excellent definitions focus on the motive behind ministry. But when it comes to understanding what kinds of activities can be ministry, a brief Greek word study may shed some light.*

The word minister *or* ministry *in the New Testament, particularly in the King James Version, is in the original Greek usually some form of the word* diakonia. *To get an idea of what* diakonia *really means, we will compare some verses where this word is translated "minister" or "ministry" in the King James Version with those same verses in a modern translation. By listening to both versions, see whether you can figure out how the word* diakonia *is translated in the modern version.*

Next, ask for volunteers to read the verses of Scripture listed below, first in the King James Version, then in a modern translation. If you have time you might ask for the reading of a second modern translation. The words found in modern translations follow the references. Jot these down on your chalkboard or newsprint as people identify them.

- Matthew 20:26, 28 (servant, serve)
- Acts 13:5 (assistant, helper)
- 1 Peter 4:10 (serve)
- Ephesians 4:12 (service, ministry. Note: The Revised Standard Version and the New Revised Standard Version retain the word *ministry* in this verse.)

Ask: *So what does* diakonia *mean?* (Service.) To minister is simply to serve. Once we understand this, we have the key to understanding how we can minister through our work.

Activity 5

What Makes a Job a Ministry? (8–12 min.)

Ask for a volunteer to read the section of chapter 4 headed "Test #1: Does Your Work Meet Needs?" As the person is reading, write on the chalkboard or newsprint (or have it written on newsprint before the session): "What need do you meet through your work?"

Next, ask for volunteers to read the following section—"Test #2: Do You Have a Servant Spirit?"—and the first three paragraphs under "The Recipients of Your Service." As these passages are being read, write on the board or newsprint: "What helps, or could help, to remind you daily of whom you are serving?"

Finally, ask someone to read the section of the chapter headed "Beyond the Job Description." As this passage is being read, write on the board or newsprint: "What opportunities does your work give you to respond to needs (minister) beyond what your job requires you to do?"

If you feel it is needed, you can quickly summarize the points made in the portions of the chapter that have been read aloud.

Activity 6

Sharing and Prayer (6–10 min.)

Form groups of three or four. Have each person share with his or her group answers to the three questions you have written on the chalkboard or newsprint. After all of its members have shared their answers to the questions, each group should close with prayer. Suggest that each person pray aloud for the ministry of the person on his or her left.

Reflecting and Looking Ahead

Were the ideas in this session new to many in your group? Did you feel that the participants were able to apply these principles to their own work situations?

One of the most difficult principles for some employed people to apply is identifying who it is they are serving by their work. It is easy to see that they are helping their employers. It is easy to see that they are providing for their families. But it may be less obvious who benefits from the products or services the business exists to provide. Was this concept clear to your group members?

Serious reflection on this week's topic will eventually lead some Christians to question whether they are in jobs that give them the greatest opportunities for ministry. That's an important question! Next week's session—on how to recognize what kind of ministry God is calling you to—will help your group members answer that question.

Discovering Your Call

Session goal: To help participants identify their spiritual gifts and discern their calls to ministry.

Materials and advance preparation needed:

1. Materials for making name tags (for example, index cards, colored markers, tape, and safety pins; or construction paper, yarn, scissors, and crayons). These should *not* be self-adhesive name tags. They will need to be taken off and put back on.
2. A gift-wrapped box and a telephone (which does not need to be connected). Before the session, display these items on a table at the front of the room.
3. Bibles
4. Chalkboard or newsprint and marker
5. Paper and pencil for each participant

Activity 1

Name Tags (2 min.)

Have materials for making name tags on a table at the entrance to your meeting room, and ask each person to make a name tag before taking a seat.

Activity 2

Introduction (2 min.)

Briefly review the key truths you have studied in the previous four sessions; then introduce this week's topic. Point out that in each of the previous four sessions you have been broadening the definition of ministry. Show how you have done that in each session. The purpose of this session, though, is to help each participant begin to focus on what specific part of God's mission in the world he or she is called to do. To achieve that objective, you will be looking at two important biblical concepts—gifts and call. Suggest that your group members think of the process this way: They will be exploring how to "unwrap their gifts" (point out the gift-wrapped box) and how to hear and answer their calls (point out the telephone).

Activity 3

How Gifts and Calls Emerge (3–5 min.)

Ask: *How can we know what our spiritual gifts are?* After participants have had a chance to comment, ask a volunteer to read the first section of chapter 5, up to the first subhead.

Before going on, make sure the group understands that a spiritual gift is visible only when it is in use. You cannot discover your gift first, then use it. Rather, you have to begin to minister, and in the process of ministering your gift emerges—you and others see it at work.

Say: *In a moment you will form small groups and try to name each other's spiritual gifts, but, before you do that, I want to point out two common hindrances to discovering spiritual gifts: (1) the confusion between the concepts of gifts and talents* and (2) excessive concern with using "technically correct" labels for spiritual gifts. Both of these problems are explained in the section of chapter 5 headed "Gifts for Everyone." Rather than asking someone to read that section, explain these two points briefly in your own words.

Activity 4

Calling Forth Gifts (8–12 min.)

Form groups of four. One person will pass his or her name tag around the group, and each of the other three persons will write on the name tag a spiritual gift he or she has seen at work in that person's life, and briefly comment on how he or she has seen this gift at work. Of course, if someone doesn't know the person well enough to name a gift, it is fine to pass. Repeat this process with each of the other three name tags.

Activity 5

The Meaning of Call (3–5 min.)

Ask someone to read 1 Corinthians 12:4–6. Point out that verse 4 mentions that God has given each of us different gifts and that verse 5 mentions that God calls each of us to different kinds of ministry or service.

Ask: *Do all the people who have the same gift also belong in the same kind of ministry?* (No, they do not. For example, one person with the gift of teaching may be a pastor, another a Sunday school teacher, another a counselor, another a writer. Each gift can be used in many different kinds of ministry.) Have those who respond explain their answers.

Explain that for the purposes of this study we are using the word *call* to mean the ministry or kind of ministry in which God is leading a person to use his or her spiritual gifts. To this point in the session you have focused mostly on gifts. Now you will shift your focus to discovering one's call.

Activity 6

Discovering Our Calls (10–12 min.)

Write the following questions on your chalkboard or newsprint (or have them written on newsprint before the session).

1. Where do you mourn with Jesus for the pain in the world?
2. What would give you joy in that painful situation?
3. If you had unlimited resources, what would you dream of doing in response to that need?
4. What would you have to risk or give up to pursue this dream?

Explain that both pain (question 1) and joy (question 2) are important clues to one's call. You might mention an example such as Dillard Taylor, who started a support group for unemployed people after he himself had experienced unemployment, or you might mention someone your group members would know. Note that one's call is often found where the world's deep pain and one's deep joy intersect.

Point out that question 3, while partly a restatement of question 2, asks us to be specific and dream big, and that question 4 asks us to consider the cost of obeying our calls.

In a moment you will ask the group to take five minutes for quiet and prayerful reflection on these questions in relation to their own calls. But, before you do that, caution the group that discovering one's call is seldom easy and may take weeks, months, or even years. While some of the participants may leave this session with clear answers to all the "call" questions, others may search for months before finding answers. The purpose of this activity is not to produce instant answers for everyone but rather to help the participants understand the process by which they can work at discerning their calls.

Check to see whether there are any questions; then ask the group to enter into five minutes of silent reflection on the four questions you have written on the board or newsprint. Some may find it helpful to jot down their answers on paper.

At the end of five minutes, suggest that those who need more time to consider their answers should write down the four questions and take them home. In the next session you will be doing more work with these same four questions.

Also encourage everyone to read chapter 5 carefully in preparation for the next session, giving special attention to the last two sections of the chapter, which discuss team ministry.

Activity 7

Sharing and Prayer (8–15 min.)

Have the participants assemble once again in their groups of four. Invite those who wish to do so to share their answers to the four questions with the others in the group. Keep an eye on the clock, and limit each person's sharing to allow others time to share. Close the session by having each person pray for the one on his or her right, especially with regard to what that fellow participant has shared.

Reflecting and Looking Ahead

While each of the first four sessions was designed to broaden participants' understanding of ministry, this session has sought to help each person focus on where his or her ministry fits into the total ministry of the body of Christ. This session, therefore, has had a stronger element of personal application than the others.

Do you feel that your group members are understanding what spiritual gifts are and how to identify their own gifts? Do they understand what a call is and how to determine what kind of ministry God is calling them to during this period of their lives?

While each of the first four sessions stands alone pretty well, sessions 5 and 6 are closely related. Session 6, in fact, is really an extension of session 5, though it introduces a new element: Once you have discovered your call, it is important to pursue that call, not alone but with others whom God has called to the same ministry.

Now may be an important time for you to check in with a pastoral staff member, to report on the responses of group members and to discuss with that person what kind of follow-through may be called for after the final session of the study. How can the congregation support people in living out their new understandings of ministry and call?

Joining the Revolution

Session goal: To help participants see the importance of team ministry and understand how to begin forming a ministry team.

Materials and advance preparation needed:

1. Before the session, write on newsprint the four "call" questions used in the last session (activity 6).
2. Before the session, prepare (or ask a group member to prepare) a three-minute summary of the section of chapter 6 headed "A Revolution in Oklahoma." This summary should *not* include the five examples of actual ministry teams at the end of that section. It should focus on (1) how the need to form ministry teams arose and (2) how the teams were formed.

Activity 1

Introducing Ministry Teams (10–12 min.)

Open with a three-minute summary of why and how ministry teams were formed at Bethany First Church (see #2 above). Then ask for five volunteers to read the five examples of specific ministries at the end of that story.

You might give participants a chance to respond to the concept of team ministry. What advantages does it have? What risks does it involve?

Activity 2

Sounding a Call (10–15 min.)

Draw the group's attention to the four "call" questions you introduced last week in activity 6. While people responded to these questions in small groups, the larger group has not yet heard all of the responses (unless your group last week was too small to break up into smaller units). You may also have some members present at this session who did not attend the last session.

Quickly review the questions; then give participants a chance to share their sense of call—where the world's deep pain and their deep joy intersect—as well as their dream of how they would like to respond to that need. How much time each person can take will depend on the size of your group.

During this activity, as people share from the deepest places within their spirits, you will be on holy ground. This is not the time to critique or ask someone to defend a sense of call. This is a time to listen with profound respect. Affirm as you are able.

List on your chalkboard or newsprint each call described—for example, ministry to abused children, outreach to young adults, church planting.

Activity 3

Forming Ministry Teams (15–20 min.)

Explain that one way to form ministry teams is to invite people to "sound their calls," to describe what ministries they believe God is calling them to. (This is what the group has just done.) Then people with similar calls can get together to explore the possibility of forming a team. Often, as someone hears another describe a call, he or she is drawn to join that ministry.

Today you will role-play the formation of ministry teams. Ask those who named the circled calls to stand and go to various parts of the room. Then ask everyone else present to choose which one of those ministries he or she is most interested in, and to join the person who sounded that call. If someone who named a call is left alone (if no one responds to that call), ask that person to join another group.

Now each group is to role-play an organizational meeting of the ministry team. Within the time allowed the groups are to see how far they can get in making the following plans:

1. What will the ministry team try to accomplish? The group may either settle on one or two goals or come up with a number of possibilities.

2. Based on the interests, experience, and spiritual gifts each person brings to the group, what might be each person's "position" on the team? What role could each play?

Obviously this task cannot be completed in ten to fifteen minutes, but this is long enough to get people to start thinking in terms of team ministry.

Activity 4

Reporting (6–10 min.)

Ask a spokesperson from each group to report on what goals the group set and to name some of the roles people would fill in the ministry team. After the reporting, acknowledge that what you have just done was role-playing. Many of the participants may not actually be called to the ministry teams they just met with. But also point out that some ministry teams have, in fact, been started with such role-playing and that there may be groups that will want to continue meeting on their own, after the study is finished, to actually organize a new ministry. Encourage any who have such an interest to follow through, and offer any personal practical support you wish to make available.

Activity 5

The Quiet Revolution (2–5 min.)

Read the Elton Trueblood quote that appears just before chapter 6. Then ask the group to imagine: *What would happen in our church if each of the ministry teams we just envisioned became a reality? What if not only the laypeople in this room, but every layperson in this church, identified a personal call to ministry and wholeheartedly committed himself or herself to obeying that call in cooperation with other believers? What would happen to this church? What kind of impact would this church make on the community?* If time permits, invite responses.

Activity 6

Closing Prayer (2–5 min.)

Ask the whole group to stand, form a circle, and join hands. As your final act together in this study, invite people to pray conversationally as they wish, and ask a specific individual to close the prayer.

Reflecting and Looking Ahead

What happened in this session is a good clue as to how much of an impact the study made on the participants. If they have been challenged, this session was probably a powerful time of sounding calls, envisioning greater possibilities for ministry, and expressing gratitude to God. If they have not been challenged, this final session may have seemed a bit hollow, with little excitement.

Do you have people in the group who are now ready to move out in ministry? Does the church need to provide practical support in forming ministry teams? What about a support group for those who want to continue working at discerning their calls and taking first steps into new personal ministries? Are there other ways the church should follow up on this study to empower participants to say yes to God's calls in their lives?

These are critical questions. Whether this study empowers its participants for ministry may depend more on what happens next than on what has happened so far.

If this study has been done in a relatively small group and significant ministry initiatives are emerging from the group, consider arranging a time for a few of the participants to report to the entire congregation on what they are learning about the nature of ministry and what kinds of ministries God seems to be calling them to. This is one way to extend the impact of the study and make it a catalyst for congregational renewal.

You may also want to consider the possibility of offering this study again—or even periodically—in the congregation. Has enough enthusiasm been generated among those participating so that others would want to take part if the study were repeated?

As a growing number of adults in your congregation begin to see themselves as ministers and fulfill their callings, your church will become the latest to join the lay ministry revolution.

Notes

1. Elton Trueblood, *Your Other Vocation* (New York: Harper & Brothers, 1952), 9.

2. R. Paul Stevens, *Liberating the Laity* (Downers Grove, Ill.: InterVarsity Press, 1985), 40–41.

3. Quoted in Elizabeth O'Connor, *Call to Commitment* (New York: Harper & Row, 1963), 102–3.

4. James Garlow, *Partners in Ministry* (Kansas City, Mo.: Beacon Hill Press of Kansas City, 1981), 61.

5. Garlow, *Partners in Ministry*, 63.

6. Richard Wilke, *And Are We Yet Alive?* (Nashville: Abingdon Press, 1986), 85.

7. Win Arn, in C. Peter Wagner, ed., *Church Growth—State of the Art* (Wheaton: Tyndale, 1986), 109.

8. Garlow, *Partners in Ministry*, video recording.

9. Names have been changed.

10. Adapted from a talk by Jim Couchenour given at Canton, Ohio, Church of the Nazarene, August 27, 1989. Used by permission.

11. Ibid.

12. Garlow, *Partners in Ministry*, 139.

13. Quoted in O'Connor, *Call to Commitment*, 169.

14. Gib Martin, as quoted in Lawrence O. Richards and Clyde Hoeldtke, *A Theology of Church Leadership* (Grand Rapids: Zondervan, 1980), 258.

15. Frederick Buechner, *Wishful Thinking: A Theological ABC* (New York: Harper & Row, 1973), 95.

16. A. Brent Cobb, *Hasten the Harvest* (Kansas City, Mo.: Beacon Hill Press of Kansas City, 1988), 73. Most of our story of the Long Beach First Church of the Nazarene's outreach in the Asian community is adapted from this book.

Eddy Hall is available to lead churchwide studies and retreats using this training program and to consult with congregations on lay ministry.

> Eddy Hall
> 101 South Pine
> P.O. Box 365
> Goessel, KS 67053
> (316) 367-2680

Gary Morsh is available to speak on lay ministry. The Center for Lay Ministry also operates a Lay Ministry Resource Center.

> Gary Morsch, Director
> Center for Lay Ministry
> 13849 S. Mur-Len, Ste. F
> Olathe, KS 66062
> (913) 764-5200

Larry Morgan, who wrote the foreword, pastors the church where this training program was piloted and is available to speak on lay ministry.

> Larry Morgan, Pastor
> First Church of the Nazarene
> 1000 N. Main
> Newton, KS 67114
> (316) 283-4270

Eddy Hall is a full-time freelance writer and editor from Goessel, Kansas. His work has appeared in nearly one hundred Christian periodicals including *Guideposts, Campus Life, Your Church,* and *Leadership.* Eddy coedits *With: The Magazine for Radical Christian Youth.* Eddy, Melody, and their five children attend New Creation Fellowship in Newton, Kansas.

Gary Morsch, M.D., a physician in Olathe, Kansas, is the founder and director of the Center for Lay Ministry, a resource center with the mission of enlisting, encouraging, equipping, and empowering laypeople to find and fulfill their ministries through the church and in the world. He also chairs Heart to Heart International, a volunteer organization dedicated to mobilizing community resources to alleviate human suffering around the world by addressing the needs of the total person. Gary, his wife, Vickie, and their four children are active in College Church of the Nazarene in Olathe, where Gary teaches an adult Sunday school class.